The Joy of Slow

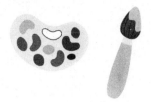

The
Joy
of
Slow

Restoring Balance and Wonder to Homeschool Learning

LESLIE M. MARTINO

A TarcherPerigee Book

an imprint of Penguin Random House LLC
penguinrandomhouse.com

Most TarcherPerigee books are available at special quantity discounts for bulk
purchase for sales promotions, premiums, fundraising, and educational needs.
Special books or book excerpts also can be created to fit specific needs. For details,
write SpecialMarkets@penguinrandomhouse.com.

Library of Congress Cataloging-in-Publication Data
has been applied for.

ISBN 9780593713181
eBook ISBN 9780593713204

Printed in the United States of America
1st Printing

Book design by Shannon Nicole Plunkett

Outdoor recreational activities are by their very nature potentially hazardous.
All participants in such activities must assume responsibility for their own actions
and safety. If you have any health problems or medical conditions, consult with your
physician before undertaking any outdoor activities. The information contained in this
guidebook cannot replace sound judgment and good decision-making, which can help
reduce risk exposure, nor does the scope of this book allow for disclosure of all
the potential hazards and risks involved in such activities.

Learn as much as possible about the outdoor recreational activities in which you
participate, prepare for the unexpected, and be cautious. The reward will
be a safer and more enjoyable experience.

While the author has made every effort to provide accurate telephone numbers,
internet addresses, and other contact information at the time of publication, neither the
publisher nor the author assumes any responsibility for errors, or for changes that occur
after publication. Further, the publisher does not have any control over and does not
assume any responsibility for author or third-party websites or their content.

This book is dedicated to my husband, Jordan, my forever partner in this beautiful, life-changing work we call parenting.

And to my children, Mya, Caden, Ethan, and Myles, who taught me the value of slow and who continue to trust me to explore it alongside them.

Contents

Foreword

Thirteen years ago, I made the unconventional decision to withdraw my oldest child from one of the best school districts in our state to—gasp!—homeschool him.

With one simple choice, I became an outlier.

I was questioned at every turn. Neighbors raised their eyebrows in concern. Friends adhered to the basic rule that "if you don't have something nice to say, don't say anything at all." Family members asked penetrating questions with equal parts curiosity and confusion.

To be honest, I don't know what possessed me either. Other than an innate desire to reclaim childhood, I had no better explanation. I wanted to do less, better. To strip away the excess. To return to simplicity. To go deep rather than wide.

And so, my son and I began.

We relished unhurried mornings with hot breakfasts and homemade play dough and then ventured outside to climb trees, draw with sidewalk chalk, or engage in pretend sword fights in the backyard.

We delved into discussions about books, history lessons, and art. We copied passages of literature into our notebooks and wrote in our morning journals. We reveled in poetry, reciting it aloud by the hearth to an audience of just us. We played hopscotch and illustrated the timeline of history on butcher paper on the back porch.

We sorted seashells from our beach days and "painted" the fence with large brushes and a bucket of water. We explored museums and art galleries and spent afternoons at local farms. We savored summer nights capturing fireflies and roasting marshmallows with friends. And on cold winter days, we read *Black Beauty* by the fire and *The Lion, the Witch and the Wardrobe* as we snuggled up at night.

There were days we worked in our math books and completed our history lessons, but there were more days when my son was so engrossed in his own projects—constructing tiny homes out of cardboard, creating imaginary worlds in the backyard, or composing short stories—that I remained in the background of his unfolding story.

On those days, I stepped in to provide a meal, a listening ear, or a kiss of encouragement, but I tried to never let schooling get in the way of his education.

This approach bewildered my friends, but it intrigued the small following I had on social media. So I invited this band of unconventional mothers from around the world to come together for a retreat about intentional motherhood. We didn't all educate or even parent our children the same way, but we all had one thing in common—whatever we did, we did it on purpose.

That small gathering turned into a beautiful community of mothers who craved a simpler life, longed to reclaim wonder, and dared to save childhood. We called it Wild + Free.

It was through this community that I met Leslie Martino.

A kindred spirit from the start, Leslie struck me as one of the most thoughtful and purposeful people I'd ever met. She was a teacher for more than twenty years, but rather than replicate the classroom at home, she allowed the "syllabus of slow" to guide her interactions with her children.

As Leslie writes, "Slow isn't ignoring traditional academic subjects. Slow is finding a balance and doing fewer things better."

When I started homeschooling thirteen years ago, I didn't know if it was possible to reclaim the wonder of childhood for my child, but I was determined to try. With no guarantees, I hedged my bets on slow.

My son's schooling was riddled with gaps, but he has filled them in as needed, because my goal was never to teach him all the subjects but to show him *how* to learn.

Choosing slow schooling with my son didn't narrow the possibilities for him but expanded them. By choosing less, we made room for more. More time for exploration, more time for questions, more time for play, more time for learning, more time for connection, more time for childhood.

Slow isn't a second-rate option to a first-class education.

Slow is an answer to the superficial.

Slow is a celebration of the sacred.

Slow is recognizing that education isn't about how fast you learn all the things but how well you understand what you learn. Slow is a mindset, an understanding that life is exciting and worth savoring.

Wonder over worksheets.

Curiosity over checklists.

Beauty over busyness.

Slow schooling offers our children the gift of time. Time to explore, play, experiment, think their own thoughts, and pursue their own passions. It gives them more time to dive deeper into subjects, to explore topics for longer times, and to be bored by inactivity, which leads to creative ideas.

Slow allows children to fully understand and appreciate what they're learning.

Slow gives them time to experience the wonder of childhood.

Slow celebrates the whole child—mind, body, and soul.

Slow schooling is taking control of the rhythms of our family's life, following the ebb and flow, and embracing the seasons and their purpose in our lives.

The idea sounds agreeable in theory, but living it out in today's world is both daring and daunting. Speed is the currency of our culture. But *not* slowing down is costing us everything.

It takes time to live and learn intentionally. One cannot rush from subject to subject and create meaningful connections. Our children grow in knowledge when they develop connections from one idea to another, and this continues to grow and expand over time.

Charlotte Mason called this the science of relations.

One could also call this an education.

For years, I could only hope that a slow education would pay off. But now, with my eldest son thriving in college and four more children coming up behind him, I know that the slow, simple, ordinary days of childhood are building not only an education for them but also a life.

Leslie embodies this better than anyone I know. She celebrates her children's curiosities and discoveries, honors their interests and passions, and looks after their developing minds with the utmost care.

When the novelist Anatole France wrote, "Nine-tenths of education is encouragement," I suspect he was thinking of Leslie Martino. (Or perhaps not, but I certainly do whenever I read his words.)

In a world that values the product of education, Leslie emphasizes the *process* as a way to honor and encourage our children's intellect, emotions, and passions. Choosing presence and connection over perfection and correction, she delights in her children's becoming.

Leslie's thoughtful approach has not only brought peace and joy to her children's education, but also inspired a community of intentional parents that desires to take this same calm and connected approach to educating their own children.

This book is a beacon of inspiration, encouraging homeschoolers, educators, and parents alike to slow down, be present, and delight in the wonder of learning.

AINSLEY ARMENT
Author of *The Call of the Wild + Free*
Virginia Beach, VA

Introduction

I have always loved the gaps, the spaces between things, as much as the things. I love staring, pondering, mulling, puttering. . . . There is so much we overlook, while the abundance around us continues to shimmer, on its own.

—NAOMI SHIHAB NYE, *CONTEMPORARY AUTHORS, VOLUME 126*

Slow down, Mama!" my daughter's little voice called to me from behind. Her three-year-old legs were tired, and she had just plopped herself down on a patch of dandelions, wanting to watch a butterfly zip around. I was probably speed walking, preoccupied with thoughts of what I should make for dinner. I turned around and walked back toward her, realizing she needed a rest. I sat beside her in silence, my eyes following the butterfly too. For the first time, I realized that it was making a bobbing motion with its body and wings (actually a figure-eight pattern) while flying. Why hadn't I noticed that before? Our eyes darted around, matching the haphazard zigzags of the butterfly's flight. I remember thinking, *I wouldn't notice half of what we did on our walks if it weren't for her persistent requests to go slower.*

That was more than ten years ago. We were taking an afternoon stroll along what is now a very familiar path. It's a walking trail that surrounds a lake in our neighborhood. Sometimes I jog while my children speed around on scooters or bicycles. At this point, we have walked along that path more times than I can count, and we are closely acquainted with what's on it. We could probably describe to you in detail landmarks along the route. Like the Spanish needle plants gathered at one particular bend on the right. Or the low camphor trees that jut out just past where the wild rabbits like to graze. Or the tortoise hole that was once just beyond the cattails, and the spot where water always collects in the field. And who could forget the home where the cat stares at us nonchalantly through the window?

As familiar as the path is, I don't think I have ever been on it without noticing something new. It has reminded me over the years that we naturally slow down when we allow ourselves to linger awhile. When we take our time, remain somewhere, or persist with something, therein lie rich opportunities to notice, appreciate, be surprised, and potentially be changed. To return to something again and again is not a waste of time. It's an expression of gratitude for time's willingness to give. On occasion, the relationship we have with this temporal gift can seem precarious. But as long as we exist inside of it, we do have some measure of control over how we experience it.

Slow schooling is an exploration of how time can be molded in partnership with the rest of the family. It is an approach to living and learning. A philosophy, or an approach to something, is usually spoken about idealistically. It paints the picture of how you would like things to be. It can exist as a beacon, there to guide your family as you go through your homeschooling years. But the day-to-day working out of an approach is messy; it's not perfect. It leaves holes and gaps in what you think creates a full picture—and it's supposed to be that way. We are complex people who need room for variation and subtlety.

In this book, I will address common questions and fears as they relate to "slow" and "education." You might feel that some ideas are unconventional. Maybe others will be more traditional or familiar. Just remember that you never have to throw the baby out with the bathwater. You can take pieces of things that speak to you and apply them as broadly or as narrowly as you like.

None of us—parents, teachers, policymakers, philosophers, students—has ever created a perfect educational system. It doesn't matter *how* you choose to school. I know that many of you reading this book are homeschool families, but I hope those of you who aren't realize that slow schooling can exist outside of homeschooling. You can take something your child is learning in school and figure out how to slow down the moments of learning that happen there, at home. You can make your home life a haven that protects everyone's internal slow meter, one that is built on connection, that sees your children for who they are no matter how they learn, and that acknowledges all their growth and development as part of a bigger picture.

Throughout the pages of this book, what all of us will have in common is that we will be confronted with the question of time: how we view it, manage it, and use it. Speed is not evil. Going fast can even be fun. But the persistent pressure to do things quickly can cause us to question if the achievement of speed comes at the expense of things way more valuable. Part One of this book will lay out why slow matters. Part Two offers practical guidance on how you might implement a slow educational approach in your home. Part Three is an endeavor to zoom out and consider how slow schooling contributes to some larger parenting aims.

For me, embracing slow has been like reestablishing a baseline. We've been realigning ourselves with what defines true quality in our lives. All these years later, I'm still taking time to sit on the ground with my children to watch butterflies. Our baseline is set. When we get off track, we just keep returning to our firm foundation. I hope you find yours too.

PART ONE

Why Slow Learning?

CHAPTER 1

First Things First

What Slow Is and What Slow Isn't

One cannot see the method; one sees the child. . . . The child qualities of which we catch glimpses are simply a part of life, like the colours of birds or the scent of flowers; they are not at all the results of any "method of education." But it is evident that these natural facts can be influenced by an education seeking to protect them, cultivate them, and assist their development.

—MARIA MONTESSORI, *THE SECRET OF CHILDHOOD*

I t was in the process of educating our four children at home that I first began to see time as a gift. I knew that there were many educational philosophies, methods, and styles, of course, but I wanted something more than that. I wanted to get to the point where I trusted my children over any system or procedure, where I could protect what I saw developing in them and participate in helping them thrive. And when I asked myself what kind of approach to education would help me observe the full spectrum of who my children were and were becoming, there was one answer that reverberated through me. I realized that having a meaningful homeschool experience involves one very bold, important act: slowing down.

The world of education tends to narrowly focus on productivity and timelines, and the homeschool community is not exempt from the pressure to succumb to a life of "faster is better," "sooner rather than later," and "hurry up and get it done." In giving in to this pressure to be and to do everything while constantly wondering if it's enough, joy is most certainly lost. Slowing down, on the other hand, is an opportunity to recapture the delight and enthusiasm that are some of the best parts of homeschooling. I no longer measure my success or our best days by how much we're doing or how much we accomplish but instead by the joy that we experience.

Most people think this sounds like a good idea in theory. In fact, over the years, I've observed a phenomenon among homeschool parents that mirrors what I've witnessed in other school settings. When their children are young, parents seem content to embrace a slow childhood. They have the desire to cultivate things like wonder, imagination, independence, and creativity, and they believe in all the benefits that a peacefully paced childhood offers. But then, as the children get older, panic sets in about what they should know to be prepared for the world beyond school. The panic creates a distorted view, and the pace of learning can become frantic and shallow, with outcomes that don't actually match the intention. Even in the younger years, fears can surface, especially in the face of learning challenges, unspoken competition with peers in the same age group, and seeing how your child measures up against all kinds of standardized assessment markers.

Or maybe you're the parent who can't possibly imagine slowing down when you can barely get enough done as it is. Nothing seems to be working well or running smoothly, motivation is low all around, and you just haven't figured out the "secret sauce" that all your friends seem to have implemented with success. Your mounting fears are rooted in your own feelings of failure.

Wherever you find yourself at this moment, keep reading. I promise you'll find something to hold on to in this book. No one is excluded from this invitation to consider a life off the fast track.

The Elements of Slow Learning

So what characterizes a slow approach to learning or schooling? I think it can be summarized by the following statements:

- Slow schooling requires that families home in on their values and adopt a meaningful practice of building deep, rather than wide, roots.

- Whether you're moving through curriculum or letting learning unfold naturally, slow schooling values deeper understanding over shallow mastery.

- You can focus on what matters most as you curate a learning environment that does fewer things better.

- Inherently, there is a healthy respect for the process of building knowledge rather than simply requiring the "right answer," because processes take time to unfold.

- Slow schooling honors a child's interests and respects the time it takes to cultivate the imagination and develop authentic skills.

- Slow schooling prioritizes doing work that is meaningful and taking the time to marvel and be amazed by the vastness of what this world has to offer—the stories of a wide array of people, places, cultures, ideas, and experiences.

- Slow schooling seeks to tackle subjects with dynamism and flexibility, using elements like spontaneity and surprise to linger a little longer with material.

- Slow schooling believes in preserving wonder for every child, regardless of their age.

- Slow schooling commits to creating the kind of space in the day that adds a sense of peace and a margin for adventure. This guards against the tendency to overschedule, to form rigid expectations, and to lead from a place of control due to fears concerning a child's academic achievement.

- This approach redefines success and broadens our understanding of what constitutes a rich learning life, recognizing that rigor and difficulty are not necessarily analogous to true and useful learning.

- Slow schooling strives for a balance of ideals when it comes to a child's growth and development.

- Slow schooling welcomes patient pursuits that replenish the soul and seeks to find beauty in the ordinary of everyday rhythms.

- Prioritizing a strong sense of connection in the family, slow schooling makes space for meaningful connection and seeks to simplify relationship-building in ways that yield profound outcomes.

- Undergirding all of these efforts is joy, because, in the end, that's what everyone will remember.

Is This Really Possible?

As I said, this all sounds great in theory, but getting to a place where you're practicing the art of slow school daily can get a little tricky. We all come to the homeschooling table with ideas and preconceived notions about what the goals of education should be, how and what our children should learn, and what our role should be.

I carry my own fair share of baggage when it comes to my views on these things. In the tradition of many Caribbean parents raising their children in America, my parents taught me the value of a solid education. Since it was thought to be, after all, a primary marker for future success, this "solid education" did not embrace concepts like doing less, taking time to figure things out, or going at your own pace. It was quite the opposite. It was more like: cooperate with and exceed the teacher's expectations, school is serious business, and good grades matter more than fun and friends. So it wasn't easy adopting slow schooling for my own children; it has been a journey of evaluating my own biases, reconciling contradicting thoughts and desires, letting go of control, and staying present to the truths my children demonstrate daily.

To add another layer of nuance, I also had about ten years as a classroom teacher to grapple with ideas about education. Fairly early on, I started to articulate many of the values I still hold today. I worked for a time in a small public school in a predominantly Black and Hispanic neighborhood in Manhattan, and though the school was often seen as unorthodox and alternative, I was acutely aware that we were doing transformative work with children. Our work was characterized by slow, patient efforts to mentor students along in their pursuits of self-directed interests and deep, rich learning. Over the years there was pushback from other educators and parents about whether this type of unconventional approach we valued really worked for the population we were serving. There were concerns that the children needed more structure, more rigor, more discipline, and all of that delivered much more quickly.

Despite the naysayers, our own informal research and other more formal studies seemed to show that we had some important insights. One source notes that the school had developed an "astonishingly rich educational program."[1] For me, a slow approach to learning at home with my children has been the true test of how much I believe in its benefits. It became something I could no longer esteem by only practicing it with other people's children. Now I had to mentally and emotionally face my own questions in a way that hit much closer to home.

Perhaps you have your own questions that you're beginning to formulate or that you've been wrestling with for a long time. Maybe you're constructing your own ideas of what the notion of "slow" could possibly mean for your home. So let's make sure we're on the same page and speaking the same language. The rest of this chapter will flesh out what slow is and what slow isn't. For every "isn't" statement, there will be a corresponding "is" statement that I hope will help to clarify this approach that *sees the child* and empowers parents to wisely manage the precious time they have with their children.

Slow ISN'T unproductive or lazy.
Slow IS quality over quantity.

In a 2004 letter titled "Slow Down: Getting More Out of Harvard by Doing Less" Harry Lewis, then dean of Harvard College, outlines for newly admitted students the benefits of making good choices while crafting a meaningful education. Advising students to use their unstructured time to figure out their true interests and to find a pace of study that works well for them, he writes:

> In advising you to think about slowing down and limiting your structured activities, I do not mean to discourage you from high achievement, indeed from the pursuit of extraordinary excellence, in your chosen path. But you are more likely to sustain the intense effort needed to accomplish first-rate work in one area if you allow yourself some leisure time, some recreation, some time for solitude, rather than packing your schedule with so many activities that you have no time to think about why you are doing what you are doing.[2]

He goes on to remind students that time is space in the day that does not need to be crammed with activity. It is in that space that creativity flourishes. Slowing down allows for a focus on the things that truly deserve attention.

When I first read that letter, I remember thinking, *Wow, here's a Harvard dean basically cosigning the idea that we don't have to feel that we're not pursuing excellence simply because we're choosing to slow down.* Slow is not about doing nothing. It's about spending time doing things that are worthwhile. With more time to focus on fewer things, it is possible to see the concept of work through a different lens. A conventional lens would reveal a bent toward valuing the quantity of work produced at the expense of quality, or results over process. But time allows for depth and nuance, which is different from performance for the sake of a grade.

Even in institutional elementary and secondary schools, educators question what has really been gained by fixating on output rather than experience and the development of the whole person. Lawrence Baines, professor of education at the University of Toledo, admonishes, "The initiatives of an extended school day, more homework, increased technology, and vigorous standardized testing, in vogue for decades, have done little to enhance achievement, promote positive attitudes, or foster good citizenship. Perhaps it is time to learn from the world, to stop thinking in terms of more and more, and consider what might be achieved by doing less."[3]

When children are working slowly enough to engage with subject matter in a meaningful way or to dedicate time to important personal pursuits, the quality of their work is often higher than if they have no real connection to what they are doing or learning. Similarly, when they have a chance to go beyond a surface-level exploration of ideas, it is qualitatively richer and more profound.

Picture this for a moment. I'm sitting around a table with a bunch of five-year-olds. I announce, "Okay, children, I want you to understand the concept of contour lines. Say it with me! I'll teach you the definition. You'll memorize it and then next week, I want you to re-tell it to me so I can make sure that you learned all about it!" Doesn't this sound a little absurd to you? Why not just hand the children a piece of paper and a pencil and begin to practice tactilely and visually perceiving the edges of an object? We could probably do that for weeks in many different ways. I'm certain that the concept could be thoroughly explored, and it would probably even begin to affect the way they saw and drew objects all the time. Whether the children could restate the definition of the word or not would be somewhat irrelevant.

As silly as that scenario sounds, it's something we do all the time with various areas of learning. We expect children to understand a concept without ever giving them time to explore it, or worse, we want them to explore it but then act as if being able to name and define it is the most important part of the experience. But there is another way. Slow implies a willingness to take the time necessary for depth of understanding and experience without feeling bad about it. Who cares about a perception of idleness when you're diligently working to integrate the most important parts of an experience?

Slow ISN'T a surefire route to "falling behind." Slow IS enough.

How many of you would say that you are your children's biggest fans? My guess would be most, if not all, of you. I get it. We applaud and cheer for them from the sidelines of sports games, lovingly brag about their milestones, and hold everything they do in high esteem. But if we're being completely honest, we're also secretly waiting for and expecting our children to reveal some sort of evidence of being truly extraordinary—not just in an "I think you're great because I'm your parent" sort of way, but in a "you're better than others in this area" kind of way. We project onto them our own fears and weighty expectations and subtly instill in them the pressure to perform. I wish we were better at trusting them to be who they are, no matter how ordinary or extraordinary.

The majority of parents I know would say that they try to appreciate each child as an individual, rather than compare them to siblings or to other children. Yet, in the same breath, they also say that they worry about their child "falling behind" academically. The problem with that is, if it isn't important to us that children do specific tasks at a specific age or follow some linear, arbitrary timeline of development for the sake of looking "standardized," then the concept of falling behind simply cannot exist.

These same parents often worry that if their child has "fallen behind," it reflects something they are doing or not doing as educators. I completely understand the fear, which stems from a genuine place of love and concern for the well-being of their child. However, negative thoughts like these might be more of an indictment against one's mindset than one's ability to educate. A mental shift is in order as we consider a different framework for thinking about growth, development, learning, and education. If we continue to offer support, resources, encouragement, guidance, and time, it will be very difficult for a child *not* to learn . . . *at their own pace.* I try to remind myself often that neither childhood nor learning is a race. Earlier is not always better. Our children are all individuals, and they are not in a race against each other, nor are they called to contend against a national standard.

Gerald Bracey, an education policy analyst, researcher, and writer who often challenged the status quo, was known for his exposés on real issues regarding testing and assessment. Among the many follies in how standardized tests are created, he named the following:

> Teachers and parents love grade-equivalents. They have such an intuitive appeal. If Suzy is in the third month of the third grade and gets a grade-equivalent of 3.3 on a test, the

teacher can tell the parents that Suzy is "at grade level," and the parents can go home thinking that Suzy is where she should be for her age. Test-makers define "grade level" as the score of the average student in a particular grade. But, like a national norm, 50% of all children are by definition below "grade level." This kind of definition can lead to a lot of mischief if, as has happened, a newspaper reports that 30% of the members of a graduating class in a high school are not reading at grade level. People who are not aware of how test publishers define grade-equivalent will assume, quite naturally, that all of the graduating seniors should be reading at grade level. And if they aren't, what on Earth is the high school doing giving them diplomas? But, to repeat, half of all students in the nation will be below grade level—by definition.[4]

As a homeschooler, you might not even use these tests (or believe in them, for that matter). The issue is that you're still indirectly applying them to how you see your child's achievement when you start to look for indicators that reveal how they measure up to their peers. The things your child "should know"—more broadly known as "academic standards"—have traditionally been set or adopted by individual states (like the Common Core initiative) and are largely developed to be uniform and highly specific. Educators are expected to cover a great deal of material in a short amount of time with no regard for thorough knowledge; the wide variety of the material masquerades as knowledge. Alfie Kohn, a well-known writer and speaker on the topics of education and parenting, notes that "the result of grade-by-grade standards, with their willful disregard of individual differences, is that some children will be branded as failures because they don't learn as quickly as their peers."[5] Yet in one way or another, these are the standards, grade levels, and development markers by which we are all abiding, no matter how we choose to school.

It's important to point out that feeling like your child is falling behind and realizing that your child has a learning challenge are not one and the same. Noticing that your child has differences in their thinking or learning is a common occurrence that has its own associated thoughts and feelings. (I'll say more about that when I discuss learning gaps.) In either case, a slow approach *is* enough because the unhurried pace allows you to truly see your child and plan your response accordingly. I know that the proverbial timetable can be a formidable tyrant that seems to keep us from the freedom to learn at an individualized, slower pace, but we can still be the bigger authority that refuses to let detrimental bureaucratic practices dictate our values.

Slow ISN'T for one specific educational philosophy. Slow IS a way to prepare for challenges.

Because people tend to gravitate toward particular educational styles, they may wonder, Can I be an unschooler, a Charlotte Mason devotee, a classical champion, a Waldorf enthusiast, or anything in between and still really embrace slow schooling? Can I use curriculum, no curriculum, an eclectic mix of curriculum, or even school online and still be in support of slow?

The answer is a resounding yes! Slow is about finding freedom and joy inside of whatever you're doing, because you have learned to *see* your child and to set your pace accordingly. You can teach the child, not the curriculum. You can use time to build moments of meaningful experience rather than see it as something to be conquered due to its impending expiration.

There really isn't one educational philosophy that can claim exclusive rights to the idea of slow. I love the way Ainsley Arment, founder of the Wild + Free homeschooling community, puts it:

> With access to ideas from around the world, homeschooling has progressed to incorporate multiple pedagogical styles, in which we're influenced by many approaches rather

than limited by one. Just as we have the freedom to home-school in the first place, we also have the freedom to adapt our approach to suit our teaching style, as well as the needs, learning styles, and personalities of our children.[6]

We tend to see educational philosophies and styles along a spectrum from "relaxed" to "rigorous" and align ourselves accordingly. Many of us have been conditioned to think that if learning something feels effortless, it can't possibly be evidence of real learning. We equate rigor with challenge. We also believe that if it wasn't a premeditated learning event, produced by our own well-intentioned efforts, it shouldn't count as true education. But I'm here today to whisper in your ear that it's all a lie. There is a different way of seeing things. We just need the confidence to look from another point of view.

Julie Bogart, homeschooler, author, and creator of the Brave Writer program, has helped me to develop a lot of this kind of confidence. There's a wonderful episode of her *Brave Writer* podcast called "Rigor vs. Relaxed Alertness" about how many parents assume that rigor is the "better" version of learning, the version where kids are learning more and doing more. She says that we have a tendency to prioritize difficulty, discipline, and meeting prescribed markers for achievement over developing in a holistic and meaningful way specific to individuals. I remember listening to this podcast episode in the car, and when I heard this statement, I actually pulled over immediately so that I could write it down: "Our goal in learning is not to get more and more comfortable with rigor and difficulty, it's to become more and more prepared for the experience of challenge. Preparation and rigor—they're not one and the same."[7]

Bogart refers to the ideal learning state as "relaxed alertness" and describes how we can facilitate it at home by helping children manage their own learning, see themselves as capable, and learn to be flexible and persistent through meaningful work. I see confronting challenges as part of the process of reading widely, thinking critically, pursuing passions, reflecting constantly, and doing difficult work, all of which are built into this slow approach. There are, in fact, lots of opportunities for children to "work hard" within slow schooling.

I couldn't help but be reminded of *The Book of Learning and Forgetting* by Frank Smith:

> Useful learning doesn't occur when we take time out of our normal lives and knuckle down to serious study. Learning is an inevitable part of our normal lives, and it only takes place, in any useful way, when we are in a normal frame of mind. The main thing we learn when we struggle to learn is that learning is a struggle.[8]

Slow ISN'T a miracle cure for learning gaps.
Slow IS a commitment to looking beyond
traditional benchmarks.

Homeschooling parents are not alone in their concerns over how much their child knows or has learned relative to how much they are expected to know or learn compared to other children their age. "Learning gaps" are the talk of school-based education, and the worry doesn't simply disappear when the setting for learning changes. But the truth is that gaps in learning are inevitable. To discuss them at large, let alone fret about them for our children, begs the questions of who has determined what this learning entails and why, how it is even measured, and what constitutes true learning in the first place. Many educators equate what is "taught" with what is "learned," but surely learning encompasses more than just acquiring information. And in this information-rich age, would it ever even be possible to know everything?

These questions make me think about the game show *Are You Smarter Than a 5th Grader?* that aired on television in 2007–2019. The basic premise of it was to see how well adult contestants remembered grade-school curricular content, answering multiple-choice questions and winning monetary prizes along the way. Part of the show's appeal was how miserably some contestants performed—what you might call their learning gaps. If we think that compulsory schooling is the best method for producing well-informed adults who remember everything that was "taught" in grade school, then I think we're seriously fooling ourselves. As a former schoolteacher who regularly promoted students to the next grade, I can guarantee that they did not have identical levels of understanding across all academic areas, nor did one child demonstrate their understanding in ways that were commensurate with every other student. Equal proficiency is unrealistic.

School officials often study how learning gaps are more broadly applied to "achievement gaps," the disparities between how much particular groups of students have achieved, or more aptly, how well these groups have "performed." To take things further, education researcher Gloria Ladson-Billings, in a 2019 interview, even describes the real problem, not as a gap but as an "education debt,"[9] a more complex situation similar to our "national debt" whereby we have left schoolchildren with a deficit that is everyone's responsibility (not the individual child's or family's) to remedy. That deficit speaks to the historic disservice done to many of our nation's children. John Taylor Gatto, author of *Dumbing Us Down*, was outspoken about the failures of mass schooling and communicated often about the importance of "rethink[ing] the fundamental premises of schooling."[10] He wrote of the perplexing role he played as a New York City schoolteacher in "teaching an invisible curriculum that reinforced the myths of the school institution and those of an economy based on caste."[11]

It seems that gaps, inconsistencies, imbalances, and inequities are prevalent everywhere. Formal schooling is no more a surefire way to rectify them than homeschooling is to avoid them. And slow schooling makes no guarantees. But here is what it does do: It invites those participating to look beyond traditional benchmarks in an effort to see and appreciate the uneven development, the deviations from typical timelines of growth, the indirect paths to getting to a destination or level of understanding, and the lopsided strengths that don't present themselves unilaterally, all from ever-changing and growing individuals.

We all have learning gaps. The key is how we interpret them. Acting as if they are only indicative of failure is unfair to the child and indicates a narrow-minded view of what being "smart" means. If we think smartness is only the ability to perform traditional school-based functions or rote learning tasks with speed and accuracy, then we'll never fully recognize a child's varied capacities. In my opinion, it is a lazy attempt that fails to notice a child's potential and to honor the fullness of who a child is.

When my son was learning about his dyslexia, he heard about the many influential people (inventors and thought leaders) who were dyslexic or who struggled with reading and still went on to do amazing things. His first reaction to his own diagnosis was, "So, you're telling me I'm a genius." That statement tickled me so much. If he was only asked to perform and produce commensurate with the rate and work of other children his age, he might not have even realized his own brilliance. But that, in fact, has not been the case.

Instead, he has had the time to pursue deep passions that have inevitably revealed his many strengths. He has had time to create, wonder, imagine, grapple with, and try out new ideas and skills at his own pace, and not before he's ready. My son has always been good with recognizing a "not yet" moment when it comes to learning many new things, and I have learned to trust his instincts when he reveals that he needs to do or learn something in a different way. I can't help but think that his self-awareness in this area has been developed through the gift of time. A slow approach has not been detrimental to him at all, and I certainly don't need research to prove it. He himself, our journey together, his confidence, and his growth are my very own empirical evidence.

Undoubtedly, parents of children with learning differences are already used to broadening their view of what a solid education entails, and it doesn't take much convincing for them to see the benefits of slow. Marianne Sunderland, a dyslexia advocate and homeschooling mother of eight, writes in her book *No More School* that "for our children who struggle inside the box of traditional education, we have no other choice than to rethink education. Either we continue pounding our 'square pegs' into round holes until they break, or we look for a system of learning that accommodates square pegs."[12] But I think this is actually necessary for *all* children, not just those with learning differences.

We typically like learning to be linear because we can more easily track it that way. If we can't somehow track or categorize learning, then we have no proof that what we're doing is "working." But who is that thinking really meant to appease? Learning can be circular and organic, and interests can be renewed or revisited over time. In fact, one of the benefits of seeing children develop gradually is that we witness the intricate layers of their learning. We can see the loops, zigzags, and connections—how natural learning *really* happens—and we can appreciate and respect it all. We can decide which gaps matter and which we might want to address in a way that doesn't feel like a desperate attempt to correct a crisis because we've neglected to take the long view.

Also, as our children grow and mature, they will become more adept at deciding for themselves which gaps they want to fill. A child who has had time to develop self-awareness and independence through meaningful pursuits and experiences, without having that time commandeered by fearful (albeit enthusiastic) adults, will be inclined to learn even when the learning is difficult or comes at a great personal sacrifice.

I'll end this point with one of my favorite quotes from Lori Pickert, author of *Project-Based Homeschooling*:

> Imagine, after fifteen years or so, you have two children who've managed to graduate with educational deficits. Which would you rather have: the child who has some holes in her

knowledge and skills? Or the child whose thinking and learning machinery is rusty from disuse? An enthusiastic and creative learner who is missing a few facts? Or the child who memorized those facts but who says, "I hate to read"? The child who is a skilled thinker and adept learner can adjust to whatever the future doles out. She can spackle in those holes in her knowledge, and she knows how to acquire skills she needs to do things she wants to do. On the other hand, the child who shoveled down his prepared education but lost his curiosity, whose interests withered away and were replaced by a general malaise and desire to just be left alone—that child has a bagful of knowledge and skills with varying expiration dates and dubious ability or desire to acquire more.[13]

Slow school is after the "skilled thinker and adept learner." It banks on quality education over a fact-filled variety consumed in an overwhelming quantity.

Slow ISN'T ignoring traditional academic subjects.
Slow IS finding a balance and doing fewer things better.

A friend told me about a conversation she had with someone who was concerned about the growing number of homeschoolers who strongly advocate for the qualities of a slow childhood. This person felt that these homeschoolers didn't care enough about foundational academics. The conversation reminded me again of the "Slow Down" letter from the Harvard dean who urged that what many see as frivolous can, in fact, be foundational. Balance is key. One pursuit doesn't have to exclude the other, and perhaps more of the frivolous (play, creativity, and freedom) is necessary to balance out a hyperfocus on the academically traditional. Striving for balance almost seems like an act of resistance against the dominant message of our time that faster is better.

It's not that traditional academic skills are unimportant, but that it isn't necessary to master them earlier and faster. People can go on to excel at them despite a later start. Will some kids naturally gravitate to reading early, doing calculus in middle school, or writing a novel before the age of ten? Yes, but that's not the same as us pushing them into it because we think that's what will guarantee a gainful future (or what will make us homeschool parent of the year).

Though it is possible to hear the word "balance" and think that you should be after "perfection," please understand how unsteady the process of finding balance can feel. Think of a hanging balance scale—the way you balance it is by fixing it when one side gets too heavy. Similarly, when you hit a season in life that feels extremely busy, there may be a lot of feelings of dissatisfaction, frustration, and tiredness before you realize it's time to make changes and balance things out with some rest or stillness. When you become so unbalanced you have to pull back and assess the damage, you can learn from it and initiate better choices. The truth is that we're always adjusting, accelerating, and decelerating when necessary.

Slow ISN'T just for young children.
Slow IS delightful learning.

Without the pressure attached to a hurried pace, I think there is an opportunity for learning to be delightful. While countless adults in a variety of settings are on a quest to make learning "fun," we need to go a little deeper than teaching as short-term entertainment. Slow schooling values learning that is rich enough to be compelling and enjoyable. With ample time, we are more willing to experiment until we find ways of captivating our learners.

We endeavor to take in and interact with information in more than one way (connecting with people, reading books, involving the body and the senses, solving problems, being outdoors, taking things in visually, playing games, relating to music, etc.). We encourage the free expression of thoughts in whatever ways feel most comfortable or instinctive. We laugh. We have a good time and seek pleasurable experiences where we're building connection while being together. There is also a sense of ownership of work with evaluative criteria that is self-imposed (by the children). In short, slow schooling is in tune with the needs of the family and adjusts the pace based on these needs, which in turn makes for a satisfying and engaging experience.

I love veteran home educator Melissa Wiley's description of her "Tidal Homeschooling":

> There is a rhythm to the way learning happens here; there are upbeats and downbeats; there is an ebb and flow. We have high tide times when I charter a boat and we set sail with purpose and direction, deliberately casting our net for a particular type of fish. On these excursions I am the captain; I have charted the course. But the children are eager crew members because they know I value their contributions. And also I provide generous rations. No stale or moldy bread on this ship: no dull textbooks, no dry workbooks. My sailors sink their teeth into fresh, hearty bread slathered with rich butter and tart-sweet jam. . . . And we have low tide times when we amble along the shore, peering into tide pools and digging in the sand, or just relaxing under a beach umbrella. The children wander off in directions of their own choosing; they dig and poke and ponder. . . . Our family enjoys both kinds of learning—the heady adventure of the well-planned fishing trip, with a goal and a destination in mind, and the mellower joys of undirected discovery during weeks at the metaphorical beach.[14]

The pursuit of joy is a high priority, and often it requires flexibility. An intuitive, responsive approach should not only be reserved for young children. All ages can benefit from slow schooling.

As children get older, parents tend to feel more responsible for homeschooling outcomes, because the end is more clearly in sight. Parents wonder if a faster pace is necessary for the purpose of accomplishing more. After all, there are CLEP tests to pass, colleges to apply to, and activities to pursue for a well-rounded appearance.

I believe that this is the time to press into our values even more strongly, so that overwhelm about what lies beyond school does not get out of hand. Teenagers also deserve a peaceful home atmosphere and an opportunity to do fewer things better. Simplicity and meaningful pursuits can still be a goal. They also deserve challenge, choice, adventure, and connection.

And let's not forget about the partnership of well-intentioned adults who can help mentor teens through how they will navigate their future, whether that includes college or not. Slow does not cease to apply to adolescents simply because parents suddenly decide that they should begin engineering their achievements. In the words of Grace Llewellyn, the writer of the classic *Teenage Liberation Handbook*, we must continue to focus on the fact that "knowledge mixed with wonder shapes your mind into the interesting, lively kind of place you'd like to inhabit for the next eighty years or so."[15] Joy is truly the key.

CHAPTER 2

Building the Foundation

The Benefits of Going Slowly

Why would I ask you to slow down? Simply because the chorus of the world is urging you and will continue to urge you to go faster.

—BILLY COLLINS, "ON SLOWING DOWN"

Are you beginning to see the advantages of a slow approach to learning at home with your children? I hope so. I can't overstate the significance of homeschooling as an opportunity to slow down and experience life at a more natural pace. While traditional schools often present accelerated learning as the reward for children who have mastered the performance-oriented behaviors of educational institutions (testing well, meeting specific imposed standards, and competing successfully for the attention and approval of the most powerful stakeholders), decelerated learning provides rewards of its own as it helps the entire family recover from overpacked schedules, information overload, and maladjustment to the demands of hurried learning.

I've observed that one of the first efforts parents usually make in embracing slow is reducing their child's involvement in extracurricular activities and spending more family time together. Some opt for more unstructured free time. Some choose private tutors to help their child step outside of the classroom tempo and increase their understanding of academic material. Others move their children from larger traditional schools to smaller public or private schools with a different set of values that better align with their needs. Still others have shifted from physical schools to schooling at home, while a sub-section of homeschoolers is deschooling, unschooling, and the like.

So what do these families gain in the process? What value do we add when we sidestep speed? This chapter will enumerate more of the benefits of going slowly. But before going further, I'd like to ad-dress one more group of parents.

A Word about Giftedness

In the homeschooling community, parents of gifted children—children who demonstrate exceptional aptitude and competence in a variety of areas—at times feel ostracized. (Note that the term "gifted" is com-monly used in educational settings for diagnostic purposes, despite some controversy.) Their children may love information and consume it in surprisingly large quantities. Other fellow homeschool families see the distinctive quality of their educational experiences and believe them to be too academic, too intense, and just overall too much.

What these outsiders usually don't see is that there is so much di-versity even within the gifted community. It would be impossible to characterize gifted children in only one way. In schools, there are pro-grams that respond to gifted children by offering them more work or advanced content in their areas of interest to satiate their hunger and readiness for increased learning opportunities. However, these pro-grams are lacking if they ignore the children's unique needs in other areas. It is a common misconception that these types of learners de-velop consistently across every area, including socially and emotion-ally. Some children demonstrate asynchronous growth.

I know that some parents of gifted children think about a slow education and wonder if it even applies to them. Fast and busy seem more closely aligned with achievement and the burgeoning academic skills that their learners typically show. If this is you, I would encourage you to reread the list of points in chapter 1 that detail how slow schooling is defined. Remember that our responsibility as parents is to recognize and truly see who our children are and to support them in every way possible. This includes their strengths, gifts, weaknesses, and struggles, along with their differences, unique abilities, and typical and atypical behavior. We must slow down long enough to notice, connect, and partner. We must support their development in a balanced way and adjust our home environments to care for all of their needs, academic and otherwise.

I don't believe this idea of slow schooling excludes any type of learner. Know your child. Accelerate and decelerate as necessary. Follow their interests for what they are, not what you want them to be. Pay attention. Maintain an atmosphere that safeguards their internal "slow"—which is to say, their peace and safety.

Mindfully Present in the Here and Now

It's safe to say that one of the benefits of a slow approach to living and learning is the ability to be more alert, responsive, and intentional. When we're mindfully present in the here and now, we're not simply rushing ahead in a rat race that is ever accelerating toward performative productivity.

In the opening of this chapter, I quoted former poet laureate Billy Collins's commencement speech at a private high school in Connecticut. In it, he cautions, "The danger in all this haste is that we ourselves will accelerate to keep pace with the speed of information, and, in doing so, we will lose sight of the real life around us, of the discreet moments of our experience, and even of the natural world, the earth which holds us in its hands."[1] His advice to that graduating class was to remain present as they moved through life. Coming from a poet, the counsel seemed fitting.

When I first read my children the picture book *Kiyoshi's Walk*, about a boy and his poet grandfather discovering where poems come from, they were most fascinated by my own stories of visiting a classroom in Japan as a child. As an exchange student expected to immerse myself in the foreign school's classroom exercises, I attempted to write my first haiku. While the form as we've adopted it into English focuses on the number of syllables in each line, the teacher emphasized that the Japanese form is more about seeing the poetic in the ordinary moments of life. What an analogy for how we can see our at-home learning experiences when we take the time to be engaged, connected, intentional, and mindful. When we slow down, we can pay better attention to the simple pleasures that are right in front of us. We can stay aware of spontaneous moments as they happen and appreciate the surprises that we might have otherwise missed, writing poetry with our lives.

Slow schooling can help us be more intentional about how we move toward goals and how we consistently incorporate our values. It helps us set a sustainable pace of daily living that integrates our ideals while also setting realistic expectations. There is latitude for peace and calm and an allowance for imperfection. Mindful presence right where we are allows us to find value in the shortcomings of today. Too often, we live solely in fast-forward, headed toward a future destination while either ignoring our current reality or lacking gratitude for our current circumstances. It's not wrong to plan for the future or set goals, but being present also helps us to recognize what's right in front of us. How can we steward the things we're responsible for if we can't even live with an awareness of them?

Intellectual Space

I have discovered that with a presence of mind, we become increasingly aware of what I like to think of as "intellectual space." To simplify, I often say that our homeschool style is one built on loving connections, rich conversations, good books, and meaningful experiences. This foundation creates room for all the deeper things we like to do: close study, investigation, sorting, reasoning, rationalizing, connecting, analyzing, evaluating, reflecting, and more. While it certainly doesn't mean that we're doing all these things every day, we have the intellectual space to do so, without a sense of pressure and speed. Slowing down allows us to form deeply rooted relationships with particular subjects or topics. And as I explained in the last chapter, deep understanding is qualitatively different from shallow learning across a wide array of topics.

This is not a new idea. As far back as the 1920s, mathematician and philosopher Alfred North Whitehead set out to reform education in the UK. He promoted the idea of teaching only a small number of subjects and attempting to weave them together seamlessly in an interdisciplinary way. He wanted students to integrate their knowledge with real life and use their imagination to play with ideas, forming connections to other ideas. He wrote, "So long as we conceive intellectual education as merely consisting in the acquirement of mechanical mental aptitudes, and of formulated statements of useful truths, there can be no progress; though there will be much activity, amid aimless re-arrangement of syllabuses, in the fruitless endeavour to dodge the inevitable lack of time."[2]

Did you catch those last few words? Attempting to do too much, pretending to master too many things, or acting as if the plethora itself is education's purpose is an "endeavour to dodge the inevitable lack of time." If slowing down is an effort to recapture what is most meaningful in the time that we have, there is an expansiveness in learning that we can experience as intellectual space for unlocking and applying ideas. A benefit of slowing down and prioritizing the values that support this pursuit is that we ease into a particular kind of educational environment, one that is spacious, unbound by time. We begin to see learning extending into life beyond the walls of our homes. It allows for meaningful experiences in constructing knowledge.

In exploring the intellectually rich and complex duties of American workers, author Mike Rose made me think a lot about how exactly the construction of knowledge takes place. Throughout his book *The Mind at Work*, he described different kinds of workers and how they develop their skills. Intellect is so often identified by measures of verbal and mathematical performance that it's easy to forget about the space needed to allow the mind to work in multidimensional ways. In one chapter, Rose wrote about a carpenter and his crew having to move slowly when encountering unfamiliar problems. "The time he took, the uncertainties and revisions, the focus of his mind on the task"[3] produced an incredibly meaningful "knowing" that was highly informed by a hand-brain connection.

Intellectual space is room not only to create meaning in complex ways but to stumble and adapt in the process. Even failures become part of a rich experience. The good news is that all these kinds of "space" can be found and recaptured by approaching time differently.

Opportunity for a Robust Learning Life

Some definitions of the word *robust* include "powerful," "vigorous," "long-lasting," and "flavorful." If I'm essentially learning through living, I suppose you could say that I want my whole life to be robust. A robust learning life is not separate from everything else. Due to its highly contextual nature, it can happen anywhere, by any means, with anyone or anything. Therefore, living and learning as an active process will differ in the ways I approach each activity. So, what can be said about engaging with the world in such a way that yields rich insights, strong connections, and resilient learners who can overcome difficulty? There are benefits to doing so slowly.

One day, after a particularly emotional coaching call in which a parent described to me the detrimental effect of the family's hurried pace on her daughter's academic development, I walked into the kitchen to make myself some coffee. Deep in thought, I opted for the pour-over method, which I enjoy precisely for its inherently slow process: instead of turning on a coffee maker and letting it brew, you manually pour hot water over the coffee grounds slowly and carefully. As I poured, I had a revelation about how, just as pour-over coffee is often the more robust beverage option, deceleration is often the more robust education option. So please bear with me as I share with you the lessons I've learned from coffee. (If you want to go grab yourself a cup of something warm to drink, my riveting analysis will be here awaiting your return.)

1. A slower pour yields more flavor.

When water filters through the coffee grounds more slowly, it produces stronger, more flavorful coffee. It would be impossible to filter all your coffee at once; even with a coffee maker, you must wait for the water to drip through the filter and into the coffee pot. In the same way, it's not important to tackle every subject, objective, or new idea all at once. In slow schooling, we can selectively concentrate on a few things at a time and focus on extracting the most flavor.

2. Technique matters but doesn't guarantee specific results.

There's a technique to the way you pour the water into the filter when making pour-over coffee; a slow and steady circular motion ensures an even brew. Likewise, to balance the needs of all the learners in our homes, we must be aware of and intentional about what kind of pace is appropriate for each one. We slow down to find it and work hard to maintain a healthy equilibrium. However, it would also serve us well to remember that although we can control the pour, we cannot completely control the time it takes for the water to filter through the coffee grounds. Even our best intentions cannot guarantee a particular response. Our children need time to process what they're learning.

3. The right filter matters.

Coffee connoisseurs in my life have taught me that different filters elicit different flavors. Although I experimented a bit at first, when I found one I liked, I stopped searching and settled on that one. In a homeschool context, you can think of your filter as all the reasons why you do what you do. Your experience will have its own unique flavor, and a slow approach will be most meaningful when you apply it to your particular circumstances.

4. The hands-on ritualistic process trains consistency.

Over time, my pour-over coffee technique got better and better, until I no longer needed to refer to my notes about the perfect water-to-coffee ratio or the correct temperature for the water. With time and practice, I was able to consistently produce a good cup of coffee. Similarly, staying present and engaged in the day-to-day ins and outs of homeschooling life trains us in consistency. Homeschooling (and parenting in general) is not always easy. Much of it is about repetition, constancy, and stability. Being consistent doesn't mean that there will never be "off" days, but committing to the process is worth it in the end.

5. The bloom of the grounds happens after waiting.

When the coffee grounds initially come in contact with water, there is a rapid release of carbon dioxide gas. While this chemical reaction is happening, the grounds cannot readily absorb the water, which is why you must pour in only a little bit of water at first and then wait for the grounds to "bloom" before pouring more. Sometimes, in all our haste to see a particular set of results, we forget to wait. To bloom is to flourish, thrive, and progress. If that blossoming requires patience on our part, then we cannot get ahead of the process. Slow and steady yields strong, powerful results.

6. Even simple equipment produces great results.

It's not just the slow speed of the water moving through the filter that matters; the equipment itself is designed specifically to accommodate a slow process. The options for pour-over paraphernalia are many, and although it has been fun to experiment with tools that make the experience easier and fancier, you can learn to produce a great cup of coffee without breaking the bank. Likewise, more than materials, curriculum, or anything extra needed to slow school, what's important is making the most out of what you already have and shifting your mindset to accommodate slow practices. In building a robust life of learning, simple will work just fine.

Well, there you have it—my review of how pour-over coffee is analogous to slow schooling. (Talk about learning something by any means! Sometimes seeing connections between things that are seemingly unrelated helps me to understand those things better.)

A Positive Emotional Environment

Do you ever think about the things that you remember from school when you were a child? I'm talking about the things that make you smile or laugh, that you couldn't forget even if you tried. My husband, Jordan, and I were once reminiscing and laughing about fun projects that we did in middle school. He remembered writing an advertising jingle with a friend about "finger-lickin' chicken." I couldn't believe that he still knew every single line of that jingle, and it amused me greatly to watch him perform it with such passion. My memory was of a group project where we came up with a spoof on the *New York Times* slogan, "All the news that's fit to print." Our slogan was, "All the news that fits, we print."

I beamed telling Jordan the story, because after all these years, I was still emotionally connected to how fun the experience felt. What was similar about both of our trips down memory lane was that neither of us was remembering isolated information or boring facts. We learned a lot about marketing and journalism through those projects, because we were doing the work of advertisers and journalists. Attached to those experiences were positive emotions, a cooperative group spirit, and fun. We can take advantage of the togetherness that homeschooling brings and create our own memorable experiences in this same spirit. Slowing down allows us to make time for connection and joy. We can make it a priority.

As my family experiences learning through all kinds of encounters with life, content, ideas, and people, because those things are inherently meaningful and relevant for us as a family, the result is that they make us happy. Joy is not something that we have to conjure up or contrive. It comes from pursuing the very things we value. Taking more time to pursue these things also gives us more opportunities to enjoy them.

To enjoy is literally to be "in joy." Slowing down gives us a chance to exist in the fullness of our experiences, whether they be pleasurable, challenging, or anything in between. It also allows for the opportunity to create a positive emotional environment that is supercharged by camaraderie and connection. Although the scientific research exists, one hardly needs it to determine whether stress and anxiety have a negative impact on learning. The emotional consequence of a positive atmosphere for learning produces more comfort, stability, and overall pleasure than it does tension, fear, or angst. A slow approach has helped my family to cultivate our relationships with one another and together to find rest, develop gratitude, and care for others.

Time for Play

I find it impossible to ignore the relationship between a positive emotional environment built from strong family connection, happiness as an outcome in the pursuit of purpose, and the work of play. In his book *The Power of Play*, David Elkind writes, "I believe that combining play, love, and work is the *means* of successful academic achievement. It is when all three are brought together that children have the best chance of learning in the context of their unique personal circumstances."[4]

Many advocacy groups in support of childhood play mention cognitive development as one of play's many benefits. And while this information is valid, I often wonder if mentioning the academic benefits is a way to justify play or to make it more easily appreciated by the masses. Children don't choose to play because it will make them smarter, but evidence of play's educative power is certainly appealing to adults. What I want to do is highlight *time for play* as a benefit of slow schooling.

Play for Children

Children play. I don't know anyone who would deny that. We've heard countless times that play is the work of a child. Most adults, without necessarily understanding exactly how it is important for their growth and development, would agree that open-ended play is good for children. But we get all bent out of shape about *how much* children should play, *where and when* play should be allowed, and *how important* it should be to everything else that children do.

Never would I have imagined that in my adult life, as both a parent and teacher, I would have to defend a child's right to play. But I have found myself doing so many times. Play has been steadily disappearing from schools, being replaced by more "rigorous" academic instruction. Parents in early-childhood classrooms are demanding to know why their children are spending so much time playing and not enough time learning their letters and numbers. I've witnessed a similar pattern among homeschoolers. Many parents wonder if they should be forgoing playtime in exchange for formal lessons, as they suspect that it is the safer option with the potential to protect them against outside scrutiny.

Slowing down doesn't just give children time to play; it also generates time for adults to notice our children's play. One day, while in the middle of spinning wildly in the living room, lost in a pretend adventure, two of my children told me that in their world, they were writing a story about two brothers. One spoke French and the other spoke English. They were on a quest to find a magic gem and had some epic escapades along the way. I was glad that I stood there long enough to notice what they were doing. I was able to appreciate how well children can build up a cache of related experiences that they then internalize through play to build deep understanding. They try out roles and ideas as they seek to make sense of new information. Unbound by rules or limiting beliefs, they aren't afraid to explore through play.

Have you noticed the same? There are so many contexts in which we can observe children playing. In describing play as an "educative drive," the Alliance for Self-Directed Education states that children play imaginatively as they think and create. They play physically as they use their bodies and explore their strength. They play "games with implicit and explicit rules." Children also play socially, interacting with others. They play through risk and adventure. They play by exploring various tools. They play with words, logic, and mathematical ideas.[5]

Play for Adolescents

What about adolescent children? Play is no less essential for them; we simply need to notice all the ways it changes. With time to play, adolescents will still be thinking creatively and problem-solving, but their developmental needs will also allow them to attempt these things with greater levels of independence. They enjoy seeking ways to express themselves and prove their capabilities. Their language, logic, math skills, and ability to use tools will take on a more complex nature. This is a direct effect of how they are developing their capacities for focusing attention, planning, making decisions, remembering, thinking about things in new and different ways, and controlling their impulses. Adolescents are discovering new interests all the time and trying to figure out their talents and aptitudes. As their peer groups become more important to them, their play may include other people, and they may begin to explore, privately and publicly, a gamut of emotions.

I love the idea of "hard fun"[6] that self-directed learning advocate Blake Boles presents in *Why Are You Still Sending Your Kids to School?* (He borrows the term from game designer Jane McGonigal.) Boles describes how play changes for adolescents, likening the process to modern gaming. Elements of gameplay, like a sense of ownership, the rewards of surmounting challenges, and sociability, lead to mental flow states that define the kind of fun teenagers are seeking. He asks an important question: "So how do you help a teenager become intrinsically motivated? How do you encourage them to voluntarily undertake challenges? How do you nurture a love for 'hard fun?' How do you get a teenager to gain skills and a work ethic, not by tricking them, but by fulfilling their genuine needs?"[7]

Captivating a teen includes elements of risk, challenge, choice, adventure, community, partnership with trusted adults, and guidelines that make sense. Naturally, we must pay close attention to how their play changes and make time for it. Realistically, that might mean incorporating into their homeschool experience things like unconventional classes, unique learning opportunities, and new approaches to how school subjects are tackled. Slow schooling allows time to explore options that make sense.

How about Play for Adults?

Like adolescents, adults maintain playful states through the ability to concentrate on a task, enjoy it for what it is, and conquer challenges that are associated with it. Why is this important in a slow schooling environment? Why should having time for play matter to adults as well as children? Allow me to explain.

In her book *The Case for Make Believe*, psychologist Susan Linn describes the correlation between "sustaining capacities for play and playfulness into adulthood and realizing our unique potential for living a satisfying life—for seeking out experiences congruent with who we really are and through which we find meaning and purpose in living." She explains that "play is our first experience with the enjoyment and challenge of intrinsic motivation" and is a way to achieve what psychologist Mihaly Csikszentmihalyi described as "optimal experience or flow." Further, she goes on to show that, different from a sense of pleasure, optimal experience goes beyond sensory gratification and is attained "with effort—when we successfully take on challenges, for instance, master new skills, or explore new ideas."[8]

Now, here's the part that really got me thinking: "For adults, the tasks that lead to optimal experience may not exactly be play, but, in addition to volition, the way we approach those tasks shares many qualities of playfulness; savoring an activity for itself, intense concentration, and a certain precariousness manifest in difficult but ultimately conquerable challenges that lead to a sense of mastery."[9]

Who wouldn't want to capture the joy of play, flow, and optimal experiences while homeschooling their children? We just need to give ourselves time to find it. Rarely discussed in the homeschooling or education world is the time we need as adults to play with our set of circumstances and turn them into "optimal experiences" while doing the work of an educator. This can happen with effort and by meeting challenges that we encounter—not all at once but in manageable doses. Instead, we usually let challenges mount and playfulness suffer to such a degree that homeschooling begins to feel like drudgery.

When was the last time you "savored an activity for itself" or "intensely concentrated" on one thing (or one subject, or one question, or one plan) for as long as you needed? How long has it been since you willingly embraced the uncertainty of something (your direction for a new year, an observation that perplexed you, an outcome you weren't expecting)? Many of us are afraid to see homeschooling as a creative or playful endeavor. That just seems too risky. But the capacity to hold the experience with a sense of playfulness could very well be crucial to our enjoyment of it.

Another reason why having time for play matters for adults is that we shouldn't stop having enjoyable activities or doing things that capture our interest and attention simply because we're homeschooling our children. To continue to play with ideas, data, tools, words, or materials is to continue to lead fulfilling lives. We need to keep experiencing the intense, purposeful, unconstrained nature of play and be free to explore the possibilities that our various interests hold. I strongly believe that our children need to see us doing the same kinds of things that we tell *them* are important for their growth.

I can't tell you how many times I've heard parents discuss how they're learning so much right alongside their children. They talk about home education as being a second chance to fall in love with learning and life. When we pursue our own interests, our children learn that adults continue to be interesting people. Being curious, creative, thoughtful, and caring is not limited to childhood. Finding ways to pursue "hard fun" while our children are pursuing their own sets a great example for them of freedom and joy in learning. We don't have to force our interests upon them or expect them to be just as interested. We can acknowledge that we too are alive, growing, and still fascinated by the world around us.

Finally, regarding playfulness, I am reminded of something I learned about adolescent play therapy from a therapist friend. For therapists who do this kind of work, a sense of humor is required. If their goal is to increase positive interactions and build connections with the children they're serving, they can't be afraid to show enthusiasm and playfulness in their approach.

I find this interesting because, in my home, as much as I love to have fun, I have never been nominated for the fun parent award. It would go to my husband every time. I have studied this phenomenon and the kind of fun my children respond to, and one thing has remained true: No matter how many times I laugh at their corny jokes or dance when they point at me for a turn to try a silly move, they respond better when I initiate the fun. Although I do this, Jordan does it much more. When time is seen as expansive rather than something we are pressed for, we are more apt to lead with playfulness. It sets the stage for bountiful opportunities for both parent and child to engage each other with honesty and acceptance in a low-pressure environment.

Less Consumption, More Slow Pursuits

Recently, my family and I vacationed in the mountains. One of my favorite things about the cabin we stayed in was that there was no television. The kids spent their days reading, playing in stick forts outside, playing board games, talking, wrestling, and hiding out in the attic loft. To me, they seemed alive and happy. Sitting out in the rocking chair on the cabin porch, sipping tea in the quiet, misty mornings, I also felt relaxed and creative, full of fresh ideas. I was able to think a lot and pray. I remember telling myself that our daily home life must be balanced by time to truly be at leisure. I wanted to return home with that thought at the forefront of my mind.

Ironically, on the long drive there, I was listening to an episode of the podcast *1000 Hours Outside* featuring Susan Linn, the same author and psychologist I mentioned above. She talked about the effects of consumerism on children, how childhood has become so terribly commercialized and adults have become so successful at instilling consumption as a chief value. She sees the instant gratification of selfish desires as a threat to childhood.

Linn explains in her book that "by letting children develop their inborn capacity for creative play, we are helping them develop skills and values that lend themselves to better stewardship of the earth and its natural resources," whereas "by preventing children from playing, we are depriving them of chances to get to know themselves in relation to the rest of the world."[10] In our commercialized culture, a sense of who you are is necessary to keep you grounded amid all kinds of distractions. You'll be less concerned with consumption and more ready to selflessly give. (I'll discuss our connection to others more in Part Three of this book.)

Slow schooling is a way to honor childhood in such a way that time can be invested in all aspects of play, playful endeavors, and "hard fun." Play is a slow pursuit. So are challenge and creativity. The benefits of going slowly include time to intentionally do what is most important. The next chapter will help you to figure out exactly what that is for you and your family.

CHAPTER 3

Core Values

Owning Your Why

*If we are going to leave a legacy for our children, then we need to be
clear on why we are doing what we are doing in the first place.*

—LEAH BODEN, *MODERN MISS MASON*

When we first started homeschooling, we had a general idea
about what our priorities were going to be and what kind of
home environment we wanted to create. My husband and I had always talked about homeschooling, and we were on the same page
about that being our intent, but there was no formal start date or
opening ceremony. We had already considered ourselves to be steeped
in home education from the very beginning as new parents, so by the
time our first child became "school age," we figured we would just go
ahead and call ourselves homeschoolers.

However, as our children continued to grow and change, we realized that a vague or general idea of what we stood for definitely wasn't
going to cut it. We needed to have a strong sense of why we were doing what we were doing, one that we had discussed together and that
existed outside of my eagerness as an educator to take on a different
kind of classroom. We needed to have a purpose that would serve us
well, especially when we encountered difficulty or experienced doubt

about whether we could really pull off such an ambitious undertaking. We also needed to establish our core values, even as we kept adapting to everyone's needs and to changing life circumstances.

Trust me, one day when you're sitting at your kitchen table in your pajamas, feeling dissatisfied while staring into the faces of restless children waiting for you to stop your latest rant about what schoolish things need to get done that day, you'll ask yourself whether how you're spending your time actually reflects your foundational beliefs about family, relationships, learning, and life. You will wonder if your actions are really lining up with what you say in your mind that you want this whole thing to be about.

So let's take this chapter to do something really important. It's time to own your why about the reasons you've opted out of institutionalized school and/or embraced slow schooling. In defining our values, we begin living and responding to life in a way that nurtures and protects them. And we don't lose time by slowing down. In fact, it's quite the opposite. We gain time to do the things we value most.

The Role of Becoming

Unfortunately, much of the root cause of our busyness as home educators is an attempt to "check boxes" that will prove to ourselves and others that we are adequately fulfilling our role. I've seen how, only a few years into the homeschooling journey, many parents admit that they feel an incredible amount of pressure to do more daily and to be more like other parents they see who seem to "have it all together." The constant comparison leads to the belief that to keep up with the masses, they have to fill their schedules, complicate their daily routines, and regularly add in new curricular options. But we have signed on to do so much more than run on a hamster wheel to keep up appearances or simply reproduce school at home. Doing more and being more pales in comparison to getting better at *becoming*.

Marc Prensky, an author and speaker well known for his ideas about digital citizenship, writes that "the real goal of education, and of school, is *becoming*—becoming a 'good' person and becoming a more capable person than when you started." According to Prensky:

> Our kids should be asking themselves: Who am I becoming? Have I become a better thinker? If so, in what ways? Am I able to do things I couldn't before? What is important to me and why? Can I relate comfortably to individuals, in teams and in virtual communities? Can I accomplish bigger, more sophisticated projects to add to my portfolio? What kind of person have I had to become to achieve these accomplishments? Can I make the world a better place?[1]

Embracing a journey to "become" has been for us a practice in measuring growth by the right metrics. It's not about piling more on our already full plates or trying to achieve greater levels of difficulty in the work we produce. We can't really do it all. As parents, we also can't possibly be *everything* that our children need. But becoming is different. It embodies the kind of purpose we want to keep central to all we do, because it's compelling enough to carry us through all of life's seasons and stages. We must know that our children are becoming, so that everything we do with them will try to support that process. However, let's not forget that we are becoming too. And getting comfortable with the process of growth amid our own shortcomings comes with the territory.

Becoming is simultaneously walking in the reality of who we are and growing through an awareness of the ability to rise to something more. We aren't simply meant to "do homeschool," to produce learned people, to check off items from a growing list of material to cover, or to be the perfect educators and parents. The recognition of who we are has a lot to do with our own expectations. As designer and author Erin Loechner puts it in her memoir *Chasing Slow*, "The answer is not to lower the expectations we have created. The answer, I believe, is to live up to the expectations we have been created for. Live up to the expectation that you are what your child needs."[2]

We must, Loechner writes, expect that we can give and show love, that we can focus on what matters, that failure is part of the process, and that our complicated, unique selves are capable of offering something amazing to our children.[3] We must also expect that every day is an opportunity to be transformed and refined by the lessons life is teaching us. A chance to be changed by the difficulties and the triumphs. An invitation to remain in process and permission to change our minds and make necessary adjustments along the way.

So, who are you becoming? Who are your children becoming? How are you becoming better? How about your homeschool experience? What can it become that it wasn't before? Let's establish some foundational principles and think about what is important to you.

What Are Your Values?

My mother once told me a story about something special that she remembered about her mom—my grandmother, or "Mamie," as I called her (in French). Mamie was a kind woman who didn't have much but always gave to others. When my mother was a child, there was one evening when her family received an unusual visit from a stranger. A woman had knocked at their door crying, pleading with my grandmother to help her find food. Mamie invited her in and asked my mother and her siblings to make the woman feel comfortable while she searched through her purse for the last bit of cash she would possess until her next payday. After retrieving the money, my grandmother ran to the kitchen to package the rest of the freshly made food that was still hot on their little stove.

Immediately after sharing all this, my mother reflected on my grandmother's actions and thought about how many similarities they shared. She realized that she also liked to care for others and make them feel loved. I wholeheartedly agreed, knowing how easy it is for my mother to make everyone who enters her own home feel welcome, loved, and nurtured. She doesn't even have to try very hard. She has a natural way of using her talents and strengths unselfishly, and she is a very skilled cook and an excellent host.

Both my mother and my grandmother demonstrated their values through their actions. What they chose to do with their resources, their time, and their gifts showed how in tune they were with things they cared deeply about—living with kindness and generosity toward others. These were values that were woven into the fabric of our family, because it was who they were and what they stood for. I saw their values being demonstrated regularly, and it affected me in the way I formed my own.

What do our actions say about us? What values do we want to live out as a family? What are the values we want to demonstrate when it comes to home education?

A tension exists between our fundamental values and what is actually happening in our home lives. It's a good tension, though, because it keeps us honest and true to those values. We have to make time and space for the things that we say we care about. Thinking something is a good idea is not the same as demonstrating it with our money, availability, or intentionality.

On an episode of Julie Bogart's *Brave Writer* podcast, psychologist Diana Hill discusses how a good way to think about values is as adverbs and verbs. We sometimes think about them as nouns, but those nouns are simply the domains in which we want the values to play out. So, for example, it's more than just, *I value my children.* It's more like, *In the domain of my parenting, I want to be present, I want to stay open, and I want to be in a heartfelt space.*[4]

Those of us endeavoring to slow school must understand exactly how what we're doing aligns with our values so that we can focus on making what's happening in our homes more meaningful, relevant, and high priority. We can move to stay in alignment with our values when circumstances shift, adjusting ourselves in the direction of what matters *most* in our parenting.

One way to tell which values matter most to us is to observe how they make us feel. When we're living out values that are important to us, we tend to feel energized and excited. When we're forcing ourselves to live out values that aren't important to us, we tend to feel drained and depleted. I spent months studying for the LSAT (Law School Admission Test) and applying to law schools before I realized how unsettled it made me feel. It wasn't just a case of testing anxiety; it was that law school simply wasn't aligned with what I found meaningful. The expectation that I *should* go to law school wasn't even mine—it was an idea that I adopted from somewhere else outside myself.

This is a great starting place to think about the things you value that will impact a slow schooling experience. What kinds of things do you love to do with your children? What motivates you and electrifies your senses? What do you long to do or wish to do more of? What do you care about most?

It might be tempting to begin thinking in terms of school subjects here: "I like to do literature studies with my children because I value books." Even if that's true, is the value of something really attached to how much we like or don't like it? Let's say you don't like doing math—that doesn't mean it's not valuable to learn. Perhaps the more important thing to consider is *what* makes something significant or meaningful to us (or how something can become so), why we care about particular activities or subjects, and what these things allow us to really do. Values are always attached to significance and meaning.

Psychologist Madeline Levine, in her book *Teach Your Children Well*, writes about defining your core values and then shifting those values into guiding principles that result in an action plan. She suggests making a list of words that are often associated with success (she uses the ones below) and ranking them on a scale from 1 to 3, with 1 being the most important and 3 being the least. She advises readers to complete the exercise truthfully and not just select things that they believe will make them appear to be a better parent. Any of these qualities can be beneficial.[5]

Popularity	Making a lot of money
Being a go-getter	Being a team player
Conscientiousness	Communicating clearly and well
Being a good problem solver	Being self-directed
Industriousness	Adaptability
Competitiveness	Having a prestigious job
Good relationships	Being collaborative
High grades	Honesty
Elite college degrees	Individuality
Being athletic	Enthusiasm
Having a family	Social consciousness
Creativity	Self-control
Independence	Physical well-being
A strong sense of self	Emotional well-being
Having power over others	Being a people pleaser
Religion	Putting in best effort
Being reflective	Being aggressive
Being generous	Curiosity
Being responsible	Confidence
Empathy	"Pillar of the community"
Being attractive	Optimism
Contributing to the community	Financial independence
Having deep interests	Having a sense of humor
Being relaxed	Resilience

From there, narrow the list down to only a few of the items you ranked most important, and use them to write a "family values statement." Then get more specific about what a given value means for your parenting and how you might guide your children toward success. For example, if you chose "Having deep interests" as a core value, you might draft the following principles (I'm paraphrasing Levine here):

- Providing exposure to a range of ideas, books, experiences, and just about anything that would draw my children's attention.

- Looking for how and when my children demonstrate that something is worth their self-directed pursuits.

- Being willing to watch the learning play out without trying to control it.

- Trusting my children's ability to choose, edit, and adjust their interests over time.

- Modeling deep interest by doing the same kind of work right alongside them.[6]

This exercise is a great way to help you define what's important to you. It addresses the hierarchy of values we espouse, whether we realize it or not, and aims to pinpoint the ones that we'd like to put energy into executing consistently. If there are core values that seem to be missing from the list, Levine encourages readers to add them.

As it relates to slow schooling, the biggest disservice we can do to ourselves and our families is to live misaligned with our values. We'll end up feeling like we never have the time for what truly matters, because we're putting too much time, energy, and attention into the things that keep us from fulfilling our highest values. So, let's be honest about what's consuming our attention and what we're tightly holding on to that isn't even important. Why are we holding on so tightly? What is at stake? What do we stand to lose by letting go? What do we stand to gain by holding on? We need to ask ourselves if the things we choose to do that constitute "school" are only enough to keep us satisfied that we're getting by or if they truly bring purpose and meaning to our lives. Our actions are informed by the values that speak to our why.

Why Are You Doing This?

During coaching calls that I conduct with parents, I ask a host of questions about their ideas, desires, expectations, and concerns that help give me insight into their experience and how I can best support them. I am always so moved by the degree to which they invite me in and allow me to partner with their extraordinary efforts.

I remember one particular video call I had with a mom I'll call Victoria, who was struggling to find meaning in what she was doing at home with her children and strongly wished to articulate a vision. It's not that she lacked proper goals or motives; her convictions about what she needed to do and why had simply become stifled by her setbacks and fears. On our second call, I read her a "why statement" that I'd synthesized from everything she'd shared with me during our first meeting. I reframed some of what she was perceiving as personal weakness to help her realize some deep desires she was holding on to for her family.

When I finished reading the simple statement, I glanced up at the screen to see her staring back at me with tears falling from her eyes. "Are you okay?" I whispered gently. After a deep breath, she told me how refreshing it was to hear her own heart communicated in a way that she could hear without filters.

If you ask a new homeschool family why they started homeschooling, they usually share a personal story that pinpoints the reason behind their initial decision. If you ask them again a few years in, their list of reasons has often grown. That's what happened to us. We started for one set of reasons but continued for reasons we didn't necessarily anticipate from the beginning. Your whys can deepen over time. They can even change or be reconstructed. But they need to be articulated and articulated often. Our whys are the foundation that we'll remember when we're seeking inspiration for the journey ahead. I can personally attest to the fact that a firm grasp on your reasons for deciding to slow school will sustain you, especially on hard days. It will help you to keep going.

Your whys are a direct reflection of your values. They are an extension of how you want to parent and apply your guiding principles to the realm of education. They give the scope of what you will call "education" and "learning" some definition. Essentially, they set you on a path and keep you moving forward.

Seeing the Way Forward

One year when I was in college, my friends and I decided to spend our spring break doing something exciting and different. It was still cold in New York, where we attended school, and we were eager for some warm weather. So, with hard-earned money saved from part-time jobs, we booked a flight to the lovely island of Saint Martin for a little sun and adventure.

Shortly after arriving on the island, our little vacation crew decided to go for a drive in our rental car. We had no idea where we were going, and at the time, GPS navigation wasn't really a thing, but we figured the island was small enough that we couldn't get lost. We had the windows down, laughing and talking loudly over the island tunes on the radio, when we noticed that our ears were starting to pop and the air was beginning to seem thin. The road was also becoming increasingly narrow. We turned down the music as oncoming cars whipped past us at full speed, despite the twisting path. At one point, the friend who was driving slowed down and tried to pull over as much as she could so that we could get a better look through the trees and get our bearings on this sloping road. Finally able to see through a clearing, we suddenly realized that we were right at the edge of a mountain. That's when the panic set in. Only a few more inches to the right and the car surely would have been sent right over the brink.

It was a moment that taught me something I'll always remember about clarity. When we were finally able to see, we not only saw the imminent danger, we also discerned what was possible and necessary for safely getting off that mountain. Our newfound clarity made it easy to decide what to do next, even though that something—tackling the cliffside descent in low gear—was difficult.

Vision brings clarity and helps us to see a way forward. Suddenly, we become aware of what might have been obstructing our view, and we have a new perspective that allows us to see past it. Vision doesn't guarantee ease, but it clarifies your purpose. With a clear vision, we can start to imagine how we want things to be, even as we're working from a plan that's not ideal. Inspiration is the motivating picture we envision of the "how." It is the stimulation that our brains need to begin figuring out the steps we must take to move forward. As my husband, Jordan, recently said in one of his own training sessions with a client, having a vision inspires the heart, and once the heart is inspired, the brain can get to work and begin to create new ideas.[7]

If you think of developing a vision as an overly idealistic practice, remember how powerful it is to hold a picture before you of what you're working toward. Alfred North Whitehead, the British mathematician and philosopher mentioned in the last chapter, had an excellent way of putting it: "When ideals have sunk to the level of practice, the result is stagnation."[8] Attaining an ideal is great, but if we park there, creativity stops and we forget the work of becoming. Vision begets more vision.

Reflect on the elements of slow schooling detailed in chapter 1. Which ones are already resonating with you? Which ones immediately cause you to imagine possibilities for you and your children? Rewrite them in your own words. What's your take so far on capturing the joy of slow? How do you want education to look for your family? Which elements of slow schooling are most closely aligned with your personal values? How do you intend to embrace them and show up every day with this new clarity that is emerging?

Sometimes it helps to take a perspective from the future. Imagine that ten years from now we're having a conversation. I ask you, "How has homeschooling been for you all these years?" and you respond, "It's been a wonderful, amazing time!" Then I say, "Really? Tell me about it!" What would you answer? What would you have to say if I asked you what the last ten years of exploring your whys looked like in your home? Now you're beginning to articulate that vision.

Meaningful Milestones

I'll never forget the time the house was really quiet in the middle of the day. I went searching for the kids and found them curled up together in a fort they had created on the bottom bunk of their bed. There was a stack of at least fifteen books sitting among them, and one child was reading aloud to the others. He was even creating funny voices for the different characters. His siblings were laughing and begging him to continue with the rest of the stack when he got to the end of that story.

It was such a sweet moment. Looking in at them, it almost felt as if we were all suspended in time. I knew all too well that soon the books would slam shut, they'd run off to play, and they'd probably be back to bickering in no time. But that moment made me feel like life was good, learning was happening naturally, and sibling relationships were strong. There my children were, joyfully living a literary life! As trivial as it may sound, it marked a meaningful milestone in how we were living our version of slow school.

When it comes to helping people figure out the manner and the means for moving forward, I use the idea of meaningful milestones to help them create a plan of approach for how they're going to put their whys (and fundamentally, their values) into action. These milestones are ways that you can imagine those whys playing out on a day-to-day basis. Essentially, they're your responses to that hypothetical question posed to you ten years in the future. They're the things you would implement to allow you to respond to that question the way you did, the things you'd like to accomplish or experiences you'd like to have that will signify you're on the right track. You can also think about them as specific actions that tie in to the principles you developed in Levine's exercise.

Coming up with meaningful milestones is not a way to plan out every little detail. It's just a way of envisioning your life, wanting the things you care about to flourish. Depending on what's in their why statements, parents I've coached have told me that their milestones include things like being involved in community outreach, seeing a project through to the end, shedding societal pressure, creating a small business, engaging in long-term travel for exposure to different cultures, spending more time outdoors, reading for pleasure without being forced, or even making a map of the neighborhood. Some of those milestones were for their children, and some were for themselves.

I think it's important to also notice these kinds of meaningful moments as they are happening, like the scene with my children that I described above. It wasn't a premeditated event or even one that I could have articulated the importance of beforehand. But when it happened, I wanted to remember that I homeschooled for moments like those, for the ability to have them in abundance and to habitually memorialize their meaning. Those spontaneous moments for you may be things like a show of progress from your child after they've struggled with something for a long time, a glimpse of empathy your child shows for someone who is hurting, a way your child has applied a newly gained skill to a different area, or evidence of a connection between the two of you that you've been working hard to build.

The milestones that we anticipate help us to stay on track with our priorities, motivating us to continue in our pursuit of what is most essential. Moments like these speak to our why. They allow us to feel like we're headed in the right direction. That's why we get so excited about the unplanned ones. They're a pleasant surprise of reassurance.

Write Your Manifesto

You have a lot to think about after reading this chapter, so here's a moment to take stock of your ideas. I'm asking you to intentionally push pause right here to write your slow school manifesto.

I like to think of this manifesto as a statement of your core values, a declaration of your homeschool whys, and an assertion of your intentions moving forward. It is something you can always refer to that will remind you of what you stand for. It can be revised as necessary, helping you to stay committed to what is most important for the season you find yourselves in. It will help you to embrace the process of growth and becoming and stay mindful of not only *what* you're doing but also *how* you're doing it.

So grab a sheet of paper, and let's begin. The sections that we will include in the manifesto are as follows:

- A why statement
- A list of values
- A summary of your vision
- A list of meaningful milestones

On the next page is a sample template that might give you an idea of how you can organize your own document. (You can download a printable one for free from my website, lesliemartino.com.)

Begin with your values. Skip down to the section after the why statement. In the heading space for each values box, write the domains you'd like to specify. For example, you might list thinking and learning, interests and passions, spiritual life, imagination and creativity, rest and leisure, or connection and relationships. There's really no wrong way to do this—it's just about what's important to you! Consider the kinds of things you admire and that truly make you perk up when you talk about them. Then, after you've written the

Slow School Manifesto

Why Statement

Value:

Value:

Value:

Value:

Value:

Value:

Vision

Meaningful Milestones

domains, go back and fill in each box underneath with the actions you want to live out associated with each one. If you took time to complete Levine's core values exercise, you might think of the heading space as the values you ranked on the list, and the box space below as the guiding principles you synthesized from them.

Next, write your why statement. Now that you've written out your values, go back to the top and fill in your why statement. A why statement is supposed to be short, sweet, and memorable. It's a reflection of all the things you say that you value. It grounds you. It reminds you why you're doing this in the first place. Even though you're working on it second, you're placing it right at the top so that it's front and center. After looking over your list of values, reflect on how they inform your reasons for slow schooling. You might begin your statement with something like, "We homeschool in order to . . ."

Now summarize your vision. Here is where you'll reformulate your own vision of slow schooling. What does it mean for you and your family? What elements are central to the experience you'd like to have? Which ones coordinate with your values? Whether it's in the form of a paragraph or a bulleted list, put all your ideas out there. This might even be the place where you acknowledge what has been standing in the way of what you want and what you've been erroneously prioritizing in your daily routine. Actively addressing these obstructions (whether that involves inner personal work or examining other outside factors) is a step toward gaining clarity and moving forward.

Create your list of meaningful milestones. What are some key experiences, opportunities, or moments you can envision as examples of ways you could live out your values and your whys? Use this section to make a list of them. Think about how your whys can be explored through the things that you do. What would it look like, and when you're doing it, how would it make you feel? What kinds of things would give you the satisfaction of knowing that you're on the right track? Attach some extra paper so you'll have space later to jot down milestones right after they occur. Use it to record events that you want

Slow School Manifesto

Why Statement

We homeschool in order to cultivate deeper family connections, to discover passions and learn skills that support them, and to develop a meaningful sense of serving others.

Value: Deep Interests

- Providing exposure to a range of ideas, books, and experiences
- Looking for how and when my children demonstrate that something is worth their self-directed pursuits
- Being willing to watch learning play out without trying to control it
- Trusting my children's ability to choose, edit, and adjust their interests over time
- Modeling deep interest by doing the same kind of work right alongside them

Value: Good Relationships

- Encouraging a strong bond with siblings so they can relate to each other on common ground
- Communicating honestly and openly
- Listening to the things my children say without discounting their feelings
- Modeling sensitivity to others' needs and self-respect about personal boundaries

Value: Being Generous

- Contributing to others' needs as a family
- Helping children perceive others' needs and seizing moments to help them show compassion
- Finding fulfillment in serving as an adult
- Having open conversations about levels of discomfort and issues that come up

Vision

Slow school will be about building knowledge through layered experiences that are relevant to personal passions. We will focus more on creative pursuits and figure out ways to do so while also having meaningful interactions with others. I think we're doing too much, and I'm seeking to rebalance our time. Less tension. More connection.

Meaningful Milestones

A family game night once a week	More time for free play
A community service project that we design and implement as a family	More weekends at home with everyone doing things they want and like to do
More variety in our nonfiction book selections	Consistently working through our least favorite subject without arguing
Intentional connections with others who are working in fields that are aligned with my children's interests	Family discussions around topics of (everyone's) interest

to always remember, things that are aligned with your reasons for staying committed to this process. Rereading those memories from time to time is good for the soul.

See my example of a completed manifesto on page 55.

You Did It! Now What?

Now take that manifesto and put it somewhere where you'll see it often. Mine is tucked right into the front of a binder I use daily. I also have it easily accessible in a note on my phone. Sometimes, when I take a solo walk around the neighborhood to clear my head and have a moment to myself, I pull out my phone and read over my manifesto. Sometimes I cry, feeling a little lost in our journey. But something in it usually catches my eye, and I feel a little more equipped to return home with new ideas about what I should do or try next.

Reread your manifesto frequently. Maybe you're the kind of person who needs to reread it daily. Maybe a monthly review works well enough for you. You determine the frequency. Just remember that it's good to regularly engage with the thinking that went behind writing it. Stay in dialogue with your family members about what it entails. Make sure that everyone is on the same page. Ask your children how they see some of those whys playing out. Communicate what's important to you and why. Ask what's important to *them*. Figure out together what you'd like to do better.

Your manifesto is a work in progress, so you must create space to not only review it but also to revise or tweak it periodically. However, it's also a tool for tweaking and revising your life when you realize that things aren't lining up. Allow it to challenge and provoke you into action whenever you realize that your life isn't a rich reflection of what you care about most.

Most importantly, be the writer of your own manifesto. If you're not influenced by the things that you personally value, you'll be influenced by what some other source thinks is important. This is your family. These are your children. You get to decide what takes precedence.

PART TWO

How to Implement a Slow Approach

CHAPTER 4

Home as Haven

Curating the Environment You Desire

Our job is to make a home for our children. Not just shelter, but a place
of refuge and covering where they feel safe to become.

—AMBER O'NEAL JOHNSTON, *A PLACE TO BELONG*

N ow that we've homed in on our values to create lasting roots that
will withstand all kinds of testing, it's time to look at how we
curate conditions in the home that will optimize the growth of the
learners within. How do we make our homes the kind of haven that
makes slow schooling possible?

When I hear the word "haven," it always makes me think of the
old fort, preserved for centuries, that my children and I once visited.
Guards were once positioned around the fort to keep watch and defend it, and the fort walls themselves were near impenetrable. It
served as a place of security from outside forces and, at times, as a
place for those within to establish an identity after fleeing various
types of danger. Those seeking sanctuary within its walls learned to
live together and create new communities. In some instances, the fort
would help the surrounding city to survive an invasion.

When I consider the home as a haven, I imagine it kind of like a fort that resists the dominant messaging of the outside throng. It defends against the influences that don't align with our true values, while at the same time intentionally creating a family culture inside. We must fiercely guard and protect the values we hold dear and simultaneously create the atmosphere that we believe will truly nourish our children. This takes work and patience. It is as much about the way that we see our children as it is about the permission we give ourselves. We need to find the freedom to create the atmosphere we want, to edit it as often as necessary, and to authentically exist in it without limitations.

When asked by an interviewer how one can incorporate family pieces into the home, interior designer Sheila Bridges says, "I think whether inherited or not, if it's something that you love you have to make room for it."[1] In a metaphorical sense, home can be a workspace, a playground, a junction, an anchor, and a place to belong. It represents the life that we shape with the people living there. To declutter, simplify, and slow down, we must focus on making room for what matters most.

Like those who curate the art for a museum—selecting, organizing, and truly looking after its presentation and well-being—we are the curators and the caretakers of our learning environments. We are the ones responsible for making room for what we love. Other people's versions of "beautiful" cannot rob us of the license we must give ourselves to find value in our unique contexts. Curating the environment is not about making it Pinterest-worthy. It's about defining what our homes will represent. Home becomes synonymous with how we want to live.

Marie Kondo, author of the bestselling book *The Life-Changing Magic of Tidying Up*, explains her method of home organization by saying that "tidying is about what you want to keep in your life, not what you want to eliminate."[2] Even after having three children and realizing the difficulty of keeping a tidy house, she still finds joy in putting her life in order by focusing on the best ways to spend her time—on the things that make the most sense for her life.[3] Professional home organizer Kay Patterson agrees: "Let's keep the things in your home that you need, are useful, and make you happy. It's that simple."[4]

I like the idea of taking inventory of our lives and all that our homes stand for and asking whether the things we find there "spark joy," as Kondo puts it. Are our homes places where joy abounds and where we regularly experience comfort and rest? What kind of life are we sharing with the people living within the walls of the safe places we're building? Home is where we hammer out our ideals and attempt to give our journeys language and meaning. It's where we contend with our convictions as we grapple with putting the things that are important to us into practice. In many ways, we are the arbiters of the home's atmosphere. We create the context in which the joy of slow occurs.

So, in curating our home environment, let us consider four elements of the home that matter greatly: visibility, encouragement, freedom from fear, and ownership of space.

A Place of Visibility

My children and I love S. D. Smith's The Green Ember series, an adventure saga full of surprising twists, epic battles, and compelling characters who happen to be rabbits. The characters have a mantra they repeat as they touch their hands to their ears, eyes, and mouths: "I will hear you with humility. . . . I will see you with generosity. . . . And I will speak to you with honesty."[5] It reminds me of our homeschool journey, which has been built by daily professions of similar principles.

Slow schooling continues to teach me how to listen without assuming that I always have the right answers. I'm continually learning to be responsive to my children's feedback and to trust the ways I've learned to hear their hearts and the ways they come alive while learning. Seeing them generously means that I look for their strengths and noble qualities, even when I'm faced with weaknesses and faults that cause me to fear and question my capabilities. I try to approach our work from a place of trust, support, and mentorship, because I believe in my children's gifts and strengths. Honest speech is the work of prioritizing our relationship and connection, because it's what matters above curriculum. We regularly exercise vulnerability as we intentionally create space for deep and meaningful connection.

In general, I've realized that we cannot do anything even remotely related to school if we haven't first cultivated an atmosphere in which each person feels loved, known, and seen—for who they are and who they are becoming. Who our children are must supersede what they know, what they can do, and how much they can produce. A place of visibility is quite simply a place where they are seen and loved for who they are.

Maria Montessori once said, "What really makes a teacher is love for the human child; for it is love that transforms the social duty of the educator into the higher consciousness of a *mission*."[6] We might not look at the work of parenting as a "social duty," but when we combine our parenting role with one of an educator, similarly, it is love that will make the experience truly transformative. In chapter 9, we will explore more deeply our role in strengthening the connection we have with our children, but for now, suffice it to say that the safe haven of home must be built from a loving foundation.

Seeing our children is part of the way that we connect with or "collect" them, a term I first heard used by Gordon Neufeld, Ph.D., and Gabor Maté, M.D., in their joint work *Hold On to Your Kids*. Daily collecting our children has to come before instructing them in any capacity. "The ultimate gift is to make a child feel invited to exist in our presence exactly as he is, to express our delight in his very being."[7] We cannot draw out quality work, appropriately pace the material we present, have realistic expectations about the work they produce, help them prepare for challenges, support their uneven development, find balance in the scope of what they are to study, or pursue delight and joy in their educational experience if the right kind of haven isn't housing it all.

Our homes must be places where our children are known and understood because they are seen. So that raises two very important questions:

- In what ways might my child be invisible?
- What are things I can try to do to make my child more visible?

You may initially be surprised or uncomfortable at the things that come up as you try to answer these questions. Sometimes we erroneously assume that because our children are compliant (whether it relates to homeschooling or not), they are well connected to us and therefore visible. But even in a loving home, a child can still feel unseen.

How often as parents do we consciously or unconsciously overlook the children who are right in front of us? It can happen easily when we are overly focused on our agenda, when we endeavor to teach a curriculum instead of the child, and when we don't look for holistic ways of meeting educational needs. Our children can be more visible in certain situations and less visible in others. Asking how and why helps us gauge how we can support them better. Do they feel like their ideas or feelings are ignored in one area but welcomed in another? Does their voice or input matter where school or learning choices are concerned? Do they shrink back when they don't feel confident? Is there another sibling who requires more of our attention? Do they blend into the background of daily life at home while we remain unaware? No matter if they are quiet, compliant, attention-seeking, or loud, we must slow down and look beyond the surface with care.

The environment we are lovingly crafting in our homes brings another story to mind: the 1941 novel *The Saturdays* by Elizabeth Enright, about a group of siblings who form an adventure club as a way to reclaim their Saturdays. In one scene, the eldest child, Mona, jumps into bed for the night.

> In a few minutes she was warm and cozy. The shade flapped against the window as it always did, and far overhead tracing its lonely path across the dark she heard the hum of the airplane. She was safe in her bed, the house enclosed her in a shell of warm security and all about, on every side, were the members of her own family who loved and understood her so well. She felt calm and happy.[8]

When I read this part aloud to my children, one of them interrupted to say that just before going to sleep, he too lies awake and thinks about how he is safe and loved. I couldn't wish for anything better.

A Place of Encouragement and Hope

We've all heard the expression "Seeing is believing." But when it comes to safeguarding our children in an environment that offers healthy expectations and developmental support, the saying should be more like "Seeing possibility is believing in potential." If we can see it, then we can figure out how to responsibly foster it.

A few years ago, my family and I visited an art gallery in New York City, where we had the pleasure of seeing some gorgeous works of art created by Makoto Fujimura. I was especially drawn to his paintings done in the traditional Japanese style of Nihonga. Around the gallery were placards upon which the artist describes the style as "slow art."[9] He explains that it took an incredible amount of time to pulverize natural minerals and prepare the pigments used for the paint. He painted in layers to create a refractive surface that allowed the paint to dry slowly, revealing a prismatic effect of color. Watching videos of him preparing the paints was as serene an experience as being in the gallery surrounded by his works.

In his book *Art and Faith*, Fujimura draws a parallel between the "beauty through brokenness" in the crushing of the mineral pigments with another cultural tradition called Kintsugi: "Kintsugi, the ancient Japanese art form of repairing broken tea ware by reassembling ceramic pieces, creates anew the valuable pottery, which now becomes more beautiful and more valuable than the original, unbroken vessel."[10] He continues:

> A Kintsugi master mends the broken tea ware with Japanese lacquer and then covers that with gold. . . . Kintsugi does not just "fix" or repair a broken vessel; rather, the technique makes the broken pottery even more beautiful than the original, as the Kintsugi master will take the broken work and create a restored piece that makes the broken parts even more visually sophisticated. No two works, done with such mastery, will look the same or break in the same way.[11]

We are all broken in different ways. Some of us may even feel that brokenness in difficult, all-consuming undertakings like parenting or homeschooling, where it feels like there are not enough wins and certainly no glory. But Kintsugi reminds me that there is great value in our brokenness and that beauty can come from shattered, difficult places. We just need to respect the process it takes to get there. In order for the broken tea vessels to become art, the artist must first recognize their potential to become something more and then begin the work of intentional, careful repair. Nurturing our children's potential requires a similar kind of work. Bringing beauty out of brokenness necessitates that we cultivate for ourselves a mindset that helps us see our children through a lens of possibility.

Seeing possibilities takes more discipline than seeing problems. It forces us to develop grit, or the ability to persevere. Grit is what makes us press on in the face of difficulty, move forward, and not give up. It allows us to see past what is difficult and to work through pain or discomfort to the fullness of what something can become on the other side.

Seeing the potential of our children is undoubtedly more difficult when we have delayed evidence of accomplishment. But in the book *Late Bloomers*, journalist and entrepreneur Rich Karlgaard makes a case for people who "[fulfill] their potential later than expected . . . frequently in novel and unexpected ways."[12] He writes, "Think about the starting point of a late bloomer. In all probability, his or her talents and passions were overlooked by a culture and educational system that measures for a cruelly narrow range of skills. It closed off the person's paths of discovery and encouragement and potential. It did not open the doors to a successful future for them because it didn't even see them."[13]

One of Karlgaard's main messages is that we can celebrate early success in balanced ways while also holding space for the possibility of proficiency and achievement that comes later. One scenario is not more important than the other. In fact, neither guarantees smooth sailing. We still need grit to continue to provide the most fertile ground for blooming.

That said, our children still need to know that we're not simply waiting for them to be something else, that we are grateful for who they are as they're in the process of becoming. Gratitude is seeing the abundance over the scarcity so that we can make the most of what we have at any given time. It carries with it an ability to let go of shortcomings, disappointments, and failures that would otherwise become obstacles. Our home becomes the place where we actively protect the vulnerabilities of our children and allow them a safe space for working out their struggles.

In her analysis of British educator Charlotte Mason's work, which describes education as an "atmosphere, a discipline, and a life,"[14] Leah Boden (aka Modern Miss Mason herself) writes about the atmosphere we cultivate in the home as parents.

If the culture of the home is created by what is intentionally formed and seen, then the tone of the home is what is heard and transferred. The atmosphere of your home is formed intentionally by how you lead as parents. It is shaped by clear, consistent communication in the intimate safe spaces where repetition and rhythm make all the difference. How we speak and what we speak about matters. What isn't said in a home is often as important as what is; silence speaks volumes.[15]

Making our homes a safe atmosphere for slow schooling has a lot to do with the ways that we interact with our children and hold space for their potential. "You can do hard things" is a refrain that is echoed often in our home. But as parents, we must never forget that persistence and resilience are not the only reasons we can do hard things. Sometimes, it's because we have an ally who looks at us, smiles, and says, "I love you, and I believe in you." That's what we do for our children.

Here are some questions to help you consider how you might cultivate an atmosphere of encouragement and hope in your home:

- What am I communicating to my child about their development?

- Where do I need to see possibilities? What broken places are begging for an opportunity to reveal beauty?

- How can I find better ways of demonstrating gratitude for who my children are right now?

- What is the fertile ground my children need for their development no matter how quickly or slowly they are blooming?

Freedom from Fear

One year, at a family gathering, my children fell subject to something we had somehow managed to avoid for a long time. It was what I think of as the "homeschooler inquisition," in which people quiz your children on a variety of subjects to test if they're, I don't know, really "schooled," perhaps. It was by no means malicious or even off-putting to the children. They happily obliged. But when it began, I felt myself tense up. I grew slightly defensive and realized that it brought up some fears I thought I had buried. I realized that I was more worried about how their potential inability to correctly answer would reflect on *me*. What would it say about me as their primary home educator?

Saying yes to slow and all that it involves takes courage. Slow implies peace, and peace requires that the tormenting ability of fear be dealt with. Fear is usually imminent whenever we perceive that everyone else is fast-tracking their way to "higher education" or similar forms of success. It looms whenever we play the dangerous game of comparison or self-consciously assume that we are failing.

We need to focus on the things that matter way more than we focus on our fears. If we use our time like the gift that it is to do the things we value, our lives will feel full for all the right reasons. The areas where we place the most attention become the most important areas to us, so let's shift our attention. Let's pursue passions, read slowly and widely, and linger over a math idea long enough to be surprised. Let's embrace the learning that comes from the rich lives that we simply go about living.

As homeschoolers, we hear statements like, "You are the expert on your child" and "You are capable of homeschooling your children," but somewhere deep within the recesses of our minds and hearts, we don't believe it. If we feel that we are somehow not capable of homeschooling effectively in any one area, then it shakes our self-assurance and presence of mind about what our priorities should be. But we must make room for our own potential: skill sets develop, capabilities change, and we can most certainly grow.

When I felt like I couldn't help a child bring a single writing piece through the revision process without tears, I didn't stay there, continuing to make the same mistakes that left both of us feeling stuck and unhappy. Instead, I decided to get some help. I sought out some new tools for how I discussed their writing with them and that supported their growing independence.

None of us would say we're the same people today that we were five years ago. After even one year of homeschooling, we have some experience to stand on. We're not static beings, destined to reap the consequences of being perpetually ill-equipped. We will never be perfect, but there are always more ways that we can get better.

Further, holding on to worry about homeschooling is probably not encouraging the home environment we're trying to cultivate. It's probably doing the opposite. In the words of homeschool mom and founder of The Peaceful Press, Jennifer Pepito, who writes all about overcoming fears in *Mothering by the Book*, "Let's take authority over our fears and self-doubt and step into a beautiful, balanced life with our children."[16] Our fears can ruin our children's sense of peace when it comes to figuring out a pace of learning that feels right. If they sense discomfort on our part, they become self-conscious about their development and how we think that they're measuring up or "performing." For example, if we say that we value deep understanding over shallow mastery but then express disappointment over our child not consuming more curricular content in less time, our messaging will be unclear, and that causes confusion. It doesn't exactly create a haven for slow schooling.

Here are some questions to help raise awareness of your personal levels of fear and freedom:

- What fears, insecurities, or roadblocks keep me from doing what I really want to be doing with my children daily?

- Have I allowed my fears to consume me? How can I shift my focus?

- Where do I lack confidence, and what skills am I looking to grow?

- Does what I say I value line up with how I communicate with my children? Am I sending a clear message?

Ideally, our homes should be the setting where, without restriction, we can explore hindrances to how we do school. We need to be able to show up as our evolving, maturing selves and do the work that enables us to overcome our fears. Like Maya Angelou famously wrote in her memoir *All God's Children Need Traveling Shoes*, "The ache for home lives in all of us, the safe place where we can go as we are and not be questioned."[17]

Ownership of Space

Now let's shift to a more practical aspect of curating a home environment, one that will also support slow schooling. Let's think about how we use our space.

One afternoon, after running around outside, all of my children settled in to read, most of them finding a quiet spot on a couch or in some corner of the house to get cozy. However, I noticed that one child went to grab his skateboard. Before long, he was rolling around on his belly with headphones on, listening to an audiobook. I heard giggles from the other room as he reacted to the story that he was hearing. At some point, he stood up, his bare feet on the skateboard, balancing while holding the device that played his book. This seemed slightly more dangerous, and I almost interrupted his listening to stop him, but he was steadily positioned and looking confident, so I decided against it. I thought it was the best example of multitasking I had seen all day. He was certainly comfortable in his own space.

Ironically, the freedom to enjoy the *home* part of homeschooling is something with which many homeschoolers struggle. Well, hold on—who am I kidding? The children don't struggle; it's the parents. We see our children with their feet up on the coffee table while we're reading aloud their science lesson, and if we're not careful, we assume that it means they're not attending to the task at hand. But what does *your* work look like when you do it at home? Are you in pajamas? Do you have more food options? Do you take outdoor brain breaks? I once got dressed for an online call from the waist up; my lower half wore some old sweatpants and a pair of fuzzy slippers.

Getting comfortable or enjoying the benefits of being at home doesn't mean that you'll never be able to dress yourself, alter your eating when necessary, or work in a different setting. The comfort also doesn't make it impossible to focus and get work done. If you feel yourself getting sleepy, you probably just change positions, seek out sustenance, or find another way to stimulate your energy. There's no need to worry the next time your children want to do math hanging upside down from a swing, type a story from their bed in pajamas, or have a snack every time they pick up a pencil. Being at home has benefits, and they are simply demonstrating a level of ownership of their own space.

So why not go all in and cultivate a unique sense of home? I recommend first observing how your family uses the space you're already in. I know how tempting it can be to think that a *different* space (i.e., anything but yours) would work better for homeschooling. We convince ourselves that we must have a homeschool room, more space for books, a local library or museum within five miles, a few acres of land for gardening, an apartment right in the city center for a more cultural experience, more space for big projects, better neighbors, a separate bedroom for each child, and so on. No matter if we live in the city or the suburbs, in an apartment, condo, RV, or house, we can come up with an excuse for why our space does not work.

I'm not saying there's no validity to those excuses. There can always be room for improvement. But the reality is that whether we think our spaces work well or not, our families are already using them in ways that fulfill particular desires for them. So we must observe the ways they use it and even recognize when their needs and desires change.

Just as we cannot assume that our spaces won't work well because they don't meet our ideals, we also cannot assume that just because our spaces look nice, they work optimally. As our children have changed and grown, we've had to edit our home to reflect the new ways they use the space and the new needs they have, while also considering our home's limitations. We've dragged bookshelves from bedroom to hallway to make room for something else, switched furniture around to suit new preferences and help our day to flow better, and rotated or replaced materials when they are no longer interesting. The point is that we've had to pay attention. We have had to be thoughtful and intentional about the educational environment and responsive to the learners who are in it.

In an engrossing chapter titled "The Kindergarten Tradition in the High School," educator Deborah Meier reminds her readers that "in kindergarten we design our rooms for real work—not just passive listening. We put things in the room that will appeal to children, grab their interests, and engage their minds and hearts."[18] Why can't we do this for children of all ages right in our own homes? (As a matter of fact, why can't we also do this for ourselves?) When it comes to doing real work that is personal and self-directed, we want certain materials or equipment at our disposal. Our children likewise need to know what is available to use and how to access it easily. If something is too far out of reach, they'll have less of a desire to use it.

So how can we intentionally support them with resources they would find valuable? Maybe we can sharpen the dull pencils and put them in an attractive container right on the dining room table. Or organize the math tools and put them in a place where the child can reach them independently. Or maybe roll some yarn and put it in a basket on your coffee table, ready to offer for finger knitting or fiddling the next time you read a story aloud. Put their ideas and plans on a bulletin board that they can see at their eye level. Actually use a craft that they've made. Put their writing in a display case or cover, and share it with the family at dinner. (See chapter 6 for more discussion of materials, choices, and self-directed work.)

My son builds a lot with Lego. He uses every inch of free space in his bedroom to store or display his builds. We added a small table to his room and are currently trying to figure out where we can put up shelves. The changes we're making reflect his interests and are an extension of how he already uses the space he dwells in. Similarly, my daughter loves plants, and she places terrariums and potted plants in places around the house that she chooses. She also loves cooking and has her own cookbooks and recipes that occupy a corner of our kitchen counter. I don't always agree with her space design or organizational choices. I sometimes have different ideas about how to make those spaces more attractive or functional. But I've learned to find a balance so that she can ultimately feel a sense of ownership and have a place to work that grabs her interest and engages her mind and heart.[19]

Our spaces will inevitably be uniquely designed to reflect the interests and needs of the people who live there. In the words of Loris Malaguzzi, founder of the Reggio Emilia Approach, "The space has to be a sort of aquarium that mirrors the ideas, values, attitudes, and cultures of the people who live within it."[20] I thought "aquarium" was an interesting word choice. An aquarium is a structure that securely holds whatever is inside. Light can filter through it because of the transparent glass, but it also reflects the colors of whatever is moving around the tank's interior. Our home offers that same security to its inhabitants. It contains safely while at the same time avoiding isolation or insulation from things outside of our own experience, and it mirrors back to us the important values and activities brimming on the inside.

Sometimes we must organize and breathe life into our workspaces so that they're more inviting for the people who use them. We want our children to feel relaxed, peaceful, and able to think clearly while they're in them. Whether we're subtracting and removing clutter or adding and providing more, intentional regard for areas in the home will naturally attract our children.

This is true not only for equipment and materials but also for how we choose to use our spaces. I used to wish that my children would spread out a bit more while working, since they tended to work right on top of each other and would end up bickering. However, I realized that they didn't spread out because *I* didn't. I placed all my things at the dining room table and conducted business from there. So I started doing things like inviting a child to do their writing with me outside, moving to another room altogether to jot down some of my notes, or calling everyone to an unexpected place to read our history book aloud. It made a huge difference. Suddenly they started being interested in these "new" spaces too, joining me or using them in refreshing ways.

Similarly, I do things for my children that I know greatly matter to *me* while I'm working. For example, when I write, I like to be near an open window. I welcome greenery. I like sunlight. When the sun goes down, I enjoy candlelight and soft ambient lighting. So when my children are doing their work at a table or computer, I light a candle for them, open a window, or place a potted plant in their line of sight. It always makes them smile or giggle and loosen up a bit. Offering a snack certainly doesn't hurt either.

What kind of surrounding would beckon you to come learn or explore? What would make you feel happy to accept an invitation to stay? Is it artwork on the walls? Quality materials or tools available for the work you want to do? A clean space? A homey, lived-in atmosphere? Friendly, pleasant conversation? A feeling of warmth and acceptance?

I believe it's important to structure an environment that appeals to the humanity of all the learners who live there. In our home, we regularly interact with each other and collaborate. We take time to engage in our work without feeling rushed. As much as possible, we rely on real reasons for engaging in the work that we do, practicing all sorts of skills without pressure. We take breaks as needed from monotonous tasks with natural periods of pause and activity. We encounter all sorts of new opportunities, and we get comfortable in our familiar surroundings. The ownership we feel over our space lends to ownership of our work, and we respect the peaceful pacing that produces it.

This is how we live. These are all things we choose to do, ways we try to exist. Curating an environment with these things in mind is a combination of what we put in our space and how we use our space, along with who we choose to be and how we choose to love those who inhabit the space. Home should be a place that spurs us toward purpose, a place that represents the ways that we pursue what's most important. It's an environment that should reflect what we hope to accomplish and the connections we want to nurture.

Here are some final questions to help you consider the practical ways that you use your home space:

- What are my children's interests? How are they reflected in the home?

- How do my children use the different spaces in the home? What's working well? What's not working well?

- How can I support how they are already using the space around them? What are their needs?

- Who owns the various spaces in our house? How can I tell?

- When I survey our home, what stands out as important? What's the overall feeling it gives off?

- What do I need for a space to feel inviting? What do my children need?

- What aspects of our home does my family most enjoy?

CHAPTER 5

Establishing Routines

Designing a Daily Flow That
Celebrates Slow Practices

*Time is a juggernaut. It makes you feel like you're
time traveling even when you're not.*

—NIKKI GRIMES

Every single morning, my daughter wakes up early before her siblings to walk the dog. It doesn't matter that I'm usually up too, sitting quietly at the table, sipping some coffee or tea. She says good morning, gives me a big squeeze, and then goes about doing something she sees as her responsibility. She greets and cuddles the dog, who is excited and expecting her arrival. She snaps on the leash while the dog sits at attention, waiting for the command to follow after she opens the front door. Did I mention that my daughter trained the dog too? Pretty awesome, right? You might be wondering how we got her to do all that. Well, the short answer is, we didn't.

My daughter has always loved animals, especially dogs. For many years, she and her siblings would beg us to get one for a pet. When she was younger, she had an opportunity to visit a local service dog facility where she learned all about how these incredible animals help people with disabilities live more independent lives. She learned about various settings where canines were used for therapy and companionship. To say she fell in love would be an understatement.

After that experience, she dedicated much of her free time to learning about dogs. I remember at one point being surprised by the great deal of information she would rattle off about breeds that we would randomly pass on the street. She endlessly researched all aspects of the field of dog training, including the dogs, their handlers, techniques, and the service dog industry.

Years went by, and that fascination did not wane. When our dog finally came along, she began attending weekly dog training classes and training the dog daily at home. She made wonderful connections with adults who work in the field, who ended up being great mentors and guides as they encouraged her to pursue related work. She also volunteered at major dog training events and made plans to volunteer with local dog rescues.

In short, my daughter's desire for a dog was deeply tied to her personal passions and independent pursuits. Her reasons for wanting to engage in this work were significant to her because of the things she valued. Caring for our family dog was another opportunity to continue doing what she loved. She created an early morning routine for herself that was an outgrowth of something she already found meaningful.

Time is a pretty powerful force to contend with. But we contend—not as in struggling against time in a contest we can't win, but as in confronting time with confidence in a bid to use it how we want. Routines help us create practices that align our time with our values. We get to design the rhythms that govern our daily lives.

Make Haste Slowly

Festina lente is a Latin term that means "make haste slowly." I first heard the term from a dear friend who had been inspired by this ancient proverb and its message of using wisdom and prudence to take important actions at opportune moments. When she told me she felt the best prudence is driven by love, it reminded me so much of the idea of slow schooling in a safe haven—an environment that furnishes hearts through patience and intentionality.

Festina lente is also the title of an essay written by sixteenth-century Dutch philosopher and scholar Desiderius Erasmus in his collection of proverbs called *Adagia*. In this essay, he sought to find connections between what different authorities (like Homer, Plato, and many others) had to say about the paradoxical maxim. It was first published in 1500, and by the ninth edition, it had become quite extensive. Erasmus wrote:

> If you consider the force and the significance which are contained in the concision of these words . . . and how applicable to every situation in life, you will soon agree that there is no other in the whole range of proverbs so worthy of use; you will feel that they . . . should recur on every monument everywhere and be spread abroad and celebrated, so that such an important thing should be so much under the public eye that no single mortal could avoid acting on it.[1]

So why did Erasmus find this idea of making haste slowly so important, with the potential for wide-reaching application? I believe it's because it carries within it the goal of demonstrating careful thought and restraint by allowing reason and intentionality to lead one's actions. "For," Erasmus wrote, "things are more likely to turn out well if they are managed with foresight and slowly maturing plans, than if they are hastened on by rash counsels."[2] What better way to manage with "slowly maturing plans" than to create routines that prompt us to carefully consider how to organize our days, that temper our ambitious plans, and that help us calibrate our speed to accommodate our maturing learners.

Routines and habits are the preparation—the slow—that comes

before the speed. The diligence and constancy necessary to create them often takes time. By the time something becomes routine, it is practiced and powerful, especially if it is built from what we value. Justin Whitmel Earley writes in his book *Habits of the Household*, "Habits are fascinating little things. They are the things we do over and over, semiconsciously to unconsciously. By definition, they are, of course, little. But the aggregate impact of habits is as big as each habit is small."[3] The repetition of essential practices, activities, and rhythms creates a scenario whereby we come to know what to expect, and we are comfortable and at ease in the flow of the familiar.

Indeed, routines allow us to hone our attention and focus for things that matter, yet they also allow us to free up new space in our minds or to reserve concentration for new challenges and tasks ahead. Stored patterns of consistently improved action help us turn mental effort toward other things that matter. The most important thing is that we get to creatively decide when and how our focus is necessary.

The Memorable Mundane and the Margin in the Middle

A big part of creating routines is doing memorable things that become traditions and that define the culture of our families. It's good to have a plan for how we want to approach or pursue something. Establishing daily rhythms and routines is putting our values into action. It's also a way of fostering greater connection through what we attempt to do daily with our children. It's a way of intentionally doing things that won't rob us of the enjoyment of it all. If we implement routines with no joy, or if we have no joy because of our routines, then we can't hesitate to look more closely at them and perhaps alter our plans. Sometimes it's not the "what" of what we're doing, but the "how." Done right, routines can help our families find freedom and joy.

But I have two thoughts about doing memorable things that I want to put out there from the start. One, we can do memorable things by becoming what I like to think of as living memories. And two, it's not just about doing memorable things but also about creating space for memorable things to happen.

Let's start with the first. We can make memories not only by inventing or adopting household practices but also by living in a way that makes us memorable, that our children won't be apt to forget. You see, all the time we spend with our children is not lost as they grow older. It's being stacked and stored like tiny grains of sand in an hourglass. That time becomes a storage of memories that has the potential to leave their hearts indelibly marked by the lasting effects of our parenthood. That's quite an extraordinary thing.

We leave those marks over stretches of time that encompass the unexpected, unusual, and momentous right alongside the familiar, common, and usual. Ordinary, everyday (some might say mundane) life can be poignant and profoundly meaningful. If we radically expect this, we can enjoy with more intensity our daily experiences. Every day doesn't have to be magical and grand. Some days will seem epic, and others will seem quite the opposite. But don't believe for a second that ordinary does not equate to great. So celebrate the small things. Make a big deal about minuscule milestones. Cherish the ordinary.

One afternoon, after a long day, I surveyed the huge mess my children had scattered across the floor and tabletops. There was work left out by someone who never cleaned up their materials. There were books piled high, including those I'd attempted unsuccessfully to read during the day. There were half-empty cups, snack plates, and even my leftover coffee from the morning. Before beginning to clean up, I snapped a photo of the chaos, which made one child ask me what I was doing. I told him that I wanted to remember how great of a day we had. He looked confused. I said that the messy scene was a picture of our mundane moments that don't seem grand at one glance. But stare long enough and what emerges is pure beauty. I saw the unique ingredients that flavored our family dynamic and encouraged meaningful memories. He smiled at me and walked away. I think he understood.

Now, let's address my second point: creating space for memorable things to happen. Too often, we do the opposite, overscheduling our days to the point that every minute is accounted for. We create pressure on ourselves when we compile a to-do list that ends up being too long and impossible to complete. "I have no time" can really mean "I have not considered what time truly encompasses."

The way we use our time is more nuanced than we give it credit for. We often only associate it with productivity and not with repose or leisure. Even connecting it with planning or processing can sometimes be a stretch for us. The truth is, our time can be used in many ways that are equally important. They include the following:

- Time to prepare

- Time to do what you've prepared for (being realistic about how much time is needed and what number of things will create a feeling of peace rather than overwhelm)

- Time for rest

- Time for passions (things that fill you up as an individual and as a family)

My advice is to have some insurance against the tendency to control every aspect of your routine. For us, that insurance is grandparents. My parents live very close to us, and my children often request to "swing by" to see them at all hours of the day. My kids also invite my parents over to listen to their stories, test their inventions, see their projects, help them with math or a language they're learning, or take a long walk with them when they get tired of being indoors.

Once, after an afternoon of hiking and nature study, we were headed back to the car, which was parked at the trailhead. I was ready to go home, start dinner, and wind down, but my children had different plans. They wanted to swing by to pick up their grandparents, bake something, and sit with them to connect over poetry. That's why we found ourselves making cornbread and pulling out poetry books at eight o'clock that night.

I am guilty of sometimes desiring perfection—of wanting plans that I've worked hard on to go just right; of wanting the routine I'm trying to establish to feel just right; of wanting no one to be whiny, tired, or hungry (and God forbid one right after the other or all at once) so that we can actually "get some things done." But when grandparents are around, I'm forced to ask myself which is more important: my children's connection with them or my control of the circumstances around which it happens. And connection wins every time.

Your insurance might be different than mine. Perhaps for you, it's natural wake-up times for your children every morning (rather than an alarm clock or a particular hour when you're dragging them out of bed). Or maybe it's a midday homeschool outing once a week that forces you to get outside of your comfort zone (or at least the four walls of your living room). Whatever it is, apply it generously. Use space in the day to simply breathe and let things be.

Pillars to Guide the Way

The first time I saw the Saint-Louis Cathedral in Fort-de-France, Martinique, I was impressed by the pillars that supported its metal frame all along its length. It was built in the nineteenth century in a tropical place known for hurricanes and earthquakes, and the pillars had to be quite strong to keep this building standing for over a hundred years. Pillars are reliable. They are strong structures that provide integral support for whatever they're holding up. And that reliability and strength provide comfort.

What are your homeschool pillars? In other words, what are the things that hold up your homeschool day? What are the elements that will support your routine in an essential way? Can you narrow them down to three? If you completed the core values exercise in chapter 3, it will probably be easier for you to translate your guiding principles and meaningful milestones into habits, or the three most important pillars for your family right now, in this season of your lives.

Another way to think of pillars is the habits that make you feel like you're moving toward your highest values each day. They're the habits that center and ground you. If you're practicing them, then you know that you're being true to yourselves and your vision for your family. Some examples would be the habit of connection and conversation, the habit of formally and informally sharing personal work with the rest of the family, or the habit of spending two hours outdoors every morning.

One of the habits that stands as a pillar in my own family is the habit of connection. In fact, in the afternoons, when we typically do literature studies and math, I refer to those times as "connection time around literature" and "connection time around math." Whether I use that terminology with them or not, my children know that there will be one-on-one time with me to converse and connect. We simply use those subjects as a context for the connection to occur. When I operate from the framework that the most important aspect of our time together is connection, it influences how I behave. It's a habit I regularly rehearse and use to gauge how our day is going. Conversely, if we have no meaningful connection during the day, our other routines don't really feel as though they have much reinforcement. The habit is a pillar that is tied to our values.

Address the Constraints and Underestimate Urgency

When I read the book *Essentialism: The Disciplined Pursuit of Less* by Greg McKeown, I immediately began drawing parallels between his concept of essentialism and how we invest our time when educating our children at home. For McKeown, "essentialism" is discerning what's important and putting energy toward those things. He discusses the necessity of having clarity about the desired outcome of anything you're trying to achieve. He calls this "essential intent," describing it as "both inspirational and concrete, both meaningful and measurable."[4] He writes that "creating an essential intent is hard" because it requires "serious discipline to cut out the competing priorities that distract us from our true intention. Yet it is worth the effort because only with real clarity of purpose can people, teams, and organizations fully mobilize and achieve something truly excellent."[5] According to McKeown, "an Essentialist produces more—brings forth more—by removing more instead of doing more."[6] As an example, he tells a business parable about a company that increased its efficiency not by *adding* new equipment or processes but rather by *removing* the main obstacle that was holding up production. He asks, "What is the obstacle that is keeping you back from achieving what really matters to you?"[7]

If we want to do fewer things better, we need to identify what individual things are holding us back from achieving that goal. There will be time to address them all eventually, but we can start with one. Is there something that we could eliminate from our daily routine? Is there a change we could make that would be the catalyst for the progress we're seeking in this area?

One obstacle might be the assumption that we need to do every single subject every day, with equal intensity, for equal amounts of time, or that we should cover every single topic known to man inside of each subject area. When I was in college, the requirements for my degree were divided across four years, and each year was divided into at least two semesters. It was common knowledge that it was impossible to fit every single course required for the degree into one semester, yet this notion doesn't always translate to elementary and secondary education. We begin to get nervous if our children skip math, science, history, or grammar for too long. Panic sets in if they don't know every single event on the timeline of history, for every single country across each and every continent. We expect breadth over depth at every turn.

We would be much better off underestimating urgency. Not everything should command our attention equally. If we treat everything as equally pressing, we reduce our own capacity to care about one thing well or to give it the critical attention that it may deserve. It's not that there aren't legitimate reasons for something to take precedence in our routine, it's just that we can't pretend to effectively address it along with every other important thing. We must slow down and prioritize where we put our energy.

Figuring Out the Right Now

What is important for you to accomplish *right now* might not be what's important next month or next year. And that's okay. What we do can be governed by seasonal shifts, literal and metaphorical. Every December, for example, my family and I abandon our regular routine in favor of one that fosters togetherness, gives us time outdoors, and greatly reduces busyness. It might help to ask yourself what you want to do daily or monthly with each child *right now*. It doesn't have to be all or nothing. You can consider what's important at the moment while incorporating your children into your planning. Communicate with them about things they would like to do, books they would like to read, or skills they want to learn. Share what you would like for them as well.

Divide your time into chunks that allow you to focus on less, rather than considering the entire year or *all* the subjects. Some people think in terms of semesters, while others prefer six-week divisions with a week off in between. Some work according to calendar quarters, and some prefer thinking in weekly or monthly increments. Whatever you choose, set realistic goals with your children about the work you want to engage in.

When I wanted to get better at sharing and discussing events happening around the world with my children, I spent time giving this goal a lot of attention. I made time for reading news articles over breakfast. I intentionally built it into conversations. I asked them if they had questions about things going on. We weren't doing this at the exclusion of all else, but to do it well, there were some months when we had to skip or shorten other things to make it happen.

When planning and considering what you will tackle *now*, you might be wondering if in order to do so, you must always keep the end in mind—if it's necessary to have a college-like understanding of all the "degree requirements" for your years of study. Perhaps, but you're also the one helping to create those requisites, so you have some latitude to do it in a way that makes sense for your family. I understand if you want to finish high school in four years or the math book by summer, but there's also comfort, peace, and power in not having finite timetables. "Finding a stopping place" doesn't always have to mean "finished." We can always create opportunities to revisit things in another semester. We can pace ourselves without regard for how fast someone else thinks we should be going. Mastery of a given area or subject often doesn't fit into a defined length of time. It has no deadline or duty to occur before the age of eighteen. (Not to mention that what most of us call mastery is more like fluency. True mastery of most subjects could honestly take a lifetime.)

Tools to Help with Planning

When establishing rhythms and routines, there are different methods of planning that might be helpful to consider. I know so many people who have been homeschooling for a while, who use some combination of several approaches. Whether this is new to you or not, before planning, I would reflect on these questions:

- What would you like to do with each child one-on-one?

- What things can you do all together?

- What things will you do with others?

- What things will each child do independently?

- What feels natural for your daily rhythms?

- When are energy levels high and low? Do those times line up with the work you're attempting to do?

- Does the workflow alternate between activities of concentration (focusing inward) and expansion (focusing outward)?

- What brings you joy? What brings your children joy?

Keep these questions in mind as you read this section on some popular and effective methods for planning homeschool schedules and routines.

Loop Scheduling

In loop scheduling, you make a list of everything you want to accomplish or things you want to focus on in a given period of time. Think of the list as a circular loop—you can stop anywhere and pick up where you left off in the loop the next day. It's not about fitting it all in every day. So, for example, a parent might choose this as their loop: math, writing, personal projects, science, and cooking. They might find that most days, they can complete the entire loop. But let's say they were only able to get through math, writing, and personal projects one day. The next day they would just start up with science, cooking, then back to math, and so on. They have the benefit of doing what's important to them and taking the time they need without pressure.

Some people make a loop of things their child can do indepen-dently, and the child keeps track of what they're doing with some sort of checklist or chart with a moveable placeholder (like math game, language game, audiobook, and copywork). Others loop subjects they'd like to get to *with* their children. Some choose to make some-thing on their list repeat because they want to do it with more fre-quency (e.g., read aloud, composer study, read aloud, history). Loop scheduling relieves the stress of not getting to everything that you planned. It's a more relaxed approach for accomplishing the same things that might be on someone else's block schedule (see below).

Another of Greg McKeown's essentialism ideas is the concept of the "buffer"—scheduling more time for an activity than you think it will take because "we can never fully anticipate or prepare for every scenario or eventuality; the future is simply too unpredictable" and buffers let us "reduce the friction caused by the unexpected."[8] A loop schedule is a way of building in buffers without being obvious about it.

Block Scheduling

In block scheduling, you figure out what days certain things will hap-pen and put them into a particular block of time. So maybe you're doing one subject twice a week (like doing history on Tuesdays and Thursdays) and another subject three times a week (like doing math on Mondays, Wednesdays, and Fridays). If you do fewer subjects at a time, you might not feel as frazzled, because you can go deeper with each subject without pressure to do everything at once. Many families organize their year into terms and block certain subjects into the days of a particular term. So maybe they're doing six weeks of art study for one term, four days a week, but then the next term they switch it up and do a unit study on the environment instead.

Remember, you can schedule or plan and still not be ruled by the clock. It is possible to loosely plan a schedule (with plenty of buffer time built in) and approach it more like a routine, without a timer going off to tell you to move on to the next activity. You can still tune into everyone's needs and joyful ways to learn. If you don't get to all that you had intended for the day, it just means that for that day, it was too much, and there are instances when that's to be expected. If there are things you intend to do but skip for one reason or the other, there doesn't have to be guilt associated with it. Be spontaneous when you need or want to be, and flow according to how you see fit.

Planning from Behind

Planning from behind is a method I first learned about from homeschooler and Brave Writer founder Julie Bogart. Essentially, it's making a record of what has already happened, not what you plan to do in the future. It's a way of capturing inspiration after it spontaneously happens. In her book *The Brave Learner*, she writes:

> I learned to *count* these educational excursions by recording them on my calendar *after* they occurred. I call this practice "planning from behind." It turned out that many of my best homeschool plans grew inside me without my conscious awareness, only to flower into a wonderful learning experience serendipitously. I noted these learning moments confident that we had been on task—deliberate, thoughtful— even if spontaneous. I had a record of how all that reflection and study had led me to some of our best homeschooling experiences.[9]

Planning from behind leaves you with a lot of space for reflecting on what happened: what went well, what went poorly, where you can provide more support, where you need to pay more attention, or what you might need to change or approach differently. This thought and deliberation can also involve your child. Each morning can be a blank slate to achieve new gains, rather than a negative balance sheet from the day before that seems to expose gaps in your progress. You can fill the slate with evidence of your idea-inspired actions, unrehearsed excitement, and organic curiosity as they happen.

Planning a Daily Flow

Planning a daily flow is a way of incorporating your top priorities for one child in a way that is intuitive with that child's needs and personal rhythms. Mihaly Csikszentmihalyi, the professor and psychologist who named and popularized the concept of "flow," wrote:

> Most of us have never had the chance to discover which parts of the day or night are most suited to our rhythms. To regain this knowledge we have to pay attention to how well the schedule we follow fits our inner states—when we feel best eating, sleeping, working, and so forth. Once we have identified the ideal patterns, we can begin the task of changing things around so that we can do things when it is most suitable.[10]

Especially as children get older, their rhythms change. The rhythm of a teen, for example, doesn't always match that of the rest of the family. When this happens, a daily flow planning style might work better than other methods. Planning a daily flow is like creating a personalized schedule for—and with—your child, while including reminders of things to do for that day. It's a plan that's adaptable to needs, circumstances, and the child's individual work. You're helping them focus their energy and more and more independently manage their time.

Of course, your child could be met with demands for their time that are inflexible, like scheduled online classes, jobs, or sports practices. In addition, you might need them to adapt to particular gathering times that you've deemed necessary for the entire family, like morning time meetings, a story you're all listening to together, or a volunteer project you're working on as a group. But even outside of these things, time is more flexible than most of us think. We can use it in creative ways that suit everyone's internal meter.

Reassess Often

No matter what method of planning we use to develop routines that help our day flow better, we must recognize daily that routines are built over time. We need to allow ourselves ample time to practice them, and we can't expect them to feel familiar all at once. We also can't necessarily anticipate how much time they will take to cultivate. We just need to focus on our plan of approach with the acknowledgment that time is needed. This requires that we reflect often on how things are going. We can use questions like these to check in with ourselves:

- Have I left room for joy in what I've created?

- Has connection with my child become strained? If so, around what subject or activity? What can I do about it?

- Who is thriving or not thriving, and why?

- Are there routines we're following that no longer serve us?

- Does what we do line up with the things we say we value?

- What's not going well and why?

- What's going well? Celebrate!

As we're sorting out the mechanics of everyday life at home, we don't have to rush headlong into patterns of activity that are devoid of meaning. Slow practices are the ones that keep us cognizant of the relationship we have with this often-elusive temporal dimension.

Routines help us arrange the hours we are faced with in ways that breathe life into us and that help us to see learning for all that it really is or has the potential to be.

In the next few chapters, we'll take a closer look at how, educationally speaking, we can take advantage of the freedoms that slowing down affords us. The pursuit of personal interests and the study of academic subjects can develop and flourish apart from haste.

CHAPTER 6

Project Time

How Self-Directed Learning Is a Key to Slowing Down

It turns out that this is how humans evolve when they are in supportive learning environments with people who trust them, and who have educated themselves about the biology and psychology of human learning. This way, self-directedness, isn't some preferred learning method, it's evidence of how learning happens.

—AKILAH S. RICHARDS, *RAISING FREE PEOPLE*

In his book *Simplicity Parenting*, educator and consultant Kim John Payne encourages parents to "write a list of things that take time. Things that can't be rushed, things that deepen over time." On that list, he anticipates the appearance of (among other things) "your child's interests, their abilities, their sense of freedom."[1] When we take the time to really listen to children and their ideas, it quickly becomes apparent that respect for their time and interests is part of the equation. To check items off a never-ending mental list of "should dos" before they graduate, homeschooling parents have been known to race their children through curricular material, sometimes at warp speed, all while demanding compliance and pleasant attitudes to boot. Whether or not the child finds the material interesting is irrelevant, so long as the parents can feel confident that they're providing a good education. As a result, parents organize their day in ways that completely ignore their children's hobbies, interests, and abilities.

Don't worry, I've been there too. I know what it's like to disregard my children's creative pursuits because I want *them* to prioritize the things that *I* prioritize, and I haven't always welcomed their input on what constitutes a quality life or a quality education. Many of us painstakingly go through the process of choosing curriculum for various subjects, saying, "Now this is what you're learning. Be happy about it!" as if those narrow categories of academic study are all that real learning encompasses.

Slowing down helps us realize that learning is happening even outside of the compartmentalized disciplines that we've imposed. Further, learning is happening all the time, and not just as a result of direct instruction. We as human beings have a capacity for learning that is immense and varied. We learn through physical activity, play, passive observation, relationships, the work of the hands, and so much more. Learning is not disconnected from our lives. We can experiment, raise bees, visit a factory, collaborate with others, sculpt, cook, construct, or spend time outdoors, and all the while we're still learning. We don't have to segment the learning, nor do we have to disqualify the life experiences.

Thus, slowing down can also be an effort to regain a sense of freedom. For your children, it's the freedom to connect with who they are as learners, workers, doers, and makers, and to figure out how this intersects with their ideas and passions. They are free to pursue areas of interest that speak to them, especially ones that develop slowly, that require time to practice, that emerge from boredom, or that benefit from a slow (i.e., not rushed) approach. For you, it's the freedom to show the values and respect you believe in by protecting one of your child's most precious commodities: their time.

Self-Directed Learning

In our home, educational freedom looks like exploring personal interests and self-directed learning. We usually spend a large part of the morning engaged in what we call "Project Time," which is basically intentional time set aside for my children to direct and manage their education. They decide what work they want to do, what materials they want to explore, and what they want to find out more about, and they make decisions about what that looks like day to day. They may decide to stay with an interest for a day, a week, or months.

Although we love all that Project Time entails, I must admit that the term doesn't quite capture all that falls under its umbrella. For starters, younger children may simply do work that they choose, rather than a "project." It's developmentally appropriate for them to stay with that choice for less time than an older child might.

Additionally, the word "project" might seem to imply that the child chooses something to study and then sees it through to the end, but the work we do during Project Time is a little too messy for such a clear-cut definition. You can't always package the learning in a pretty little box of your choosing; it will look completely different depending on who your children are and what their interests are. Nor is the child restricted to one project until completion. What if a child is juggling multiple interests at once? Often a child's work does not result in a physical "project" but rather an experience. My children's "projects" (or what they were really learning) have sometimes been difficult to describe, but the difficulty of defining what was happening was indicative of the intensity of their experiences.

Although I'll give examples of how Project Time looks in our home throughout this chapter, I want to begin by saying that there is no one correct way to do Project Time or project-based learning. You could be doing things very similarly or very differently, and it could still be an approach to learning that is, in fact, directed by the learners. Your home will have its own unique flavor of how all these ideas are implemented in your everyday lives.

In general, I think self-directed learning can be described as a life-long adventure. It's a mindset. It's the self-awareness to create your own road map for truly learning something. And what is true learning if it's not marked by independent pursuits of knowledge worth knowing? We're all lifelong learners. There is a very natural desire in all of us to observe and to wonder. We learn things we're curious about or interested in. Self-directed learning is about finding a way of discovering the world around us, and for many of us, it involves the practice of making and doing.

What is something that you wanted to learn and then decided to go about learning? Maybe it was gardening, knitting, painting, learning a musical instrument, remodeling a kitchen, or figuring out how to cut someone's hair. Think about what you did to pursue that knowledge. When I wanted to learn to paint landscapes, I got myself some quality watercolor paints, some good brushes, and some painting paper, and I got to painting. I spent time on it. I looked for classes and videos that would help me. I sought out mentors to help get me started and give me some good tips. I took lots of photos of landscapes and I tried to paint them. I dragged my supplies outdoors and tried to re-create on paper the landscapes I was seeing. I even kept a journal of reflections on my work and my thoughts about my progress.

I also got extremely interested in the art of the Florida Highwaymen, a group of twenty-six Black landscape artists who, from the 1950s through the 1970s, sold their art pieces door-to-door, out of the trunks of their cars, and on the highways of Florida's Fort Pierce area. I will sheepishly admit that I became something of a groupie. I would find exhibits that first- and second-generation Highwaymen were having all around my area and take along the kids to go have a "chat." Sometimes we even got to watch them paint. I combed the internet for their blogs, biographies, and anything I could find. I learned a whole lot of history in the process. Even though I invited my children along on this journey, it was a learning adventure that was very personal for me. All my efforts to find information, uncover hard-to-find art pieces, and locate myself inside an art form that I was developing a relationship with brought me to a new place of discovery.

If you've ever taken on a huge task in unfamiliar territory, like starting a business, creating a website, or learning a new skill, did you say to yourself, "I'd better go back to school so someone can teach me how to do this"? Maybe that's necessary in some instances, but many times, you just go about learning or discovering more on your own. It's why many adults end up working in fields outside of the degree they pursued in college. You don't always have to return to formal schooling to learn something new. Many of us in our adult lives are in some way embracing an education that we've chosen for ourselves, that we've managed and directed on our own.

Yet somehow, we have a hard time believing that it's important to give children these types of experiences too. We think we must use our time with them at home to drill them on the fundamentals so that somehow, magically, later on, they'll be "smart" about choosing their path. But I think the opposite is true. I think we need to slow down long enough to allow children to authentically develop things like perseverance, an ability to think about their thinking, an innovative mind, sophisticated systems of testing out what they know to be true, and grit. We can do this by ensuring they have lots of experience with pursuing their passions and following their interests—as children. Because their path begins now, not when they're older, and a meaningful education is meaningful now, not just to choose a career in the future. Our children are capable of self-directed pursuits; we often just don't give them enough credit.

Our Project Times are important because I believe that we all should have a right to our own ideas and our own work. Many of us are comfortable with children doing this outside of the parameters of "school," but what if this became a priority for true learning? We all want to pursue work for our own purposes. I find myself saying a lot to my children, "Pursue what you're passionate about!" because I want to see them learning and growing in the context of what really drives them.

Author, educator, and homeschooling advocate John Holt, in his book *Learning All the Time*, wrote, "We can best help children learn, not by deciding what we think they should learn and thinking of ingenious ways to teach it to them, but by making the world, as far as we can, accessible to them, paying serious attention to what they do, answering their questions—if they have any—and helping them explore the things they are most interested in."[2]

When there's a true interest, that's when the most work, activity, growth, and learning will happen. As parents, we value learning, right? We love to see our children gain new understanding. We get excited when they know something well. But truly knowing is not the same as regurgitating facts. In an endless pursuit to somehow quantify and qualify what children know, adults can often find themselves taking a very rudimentary approach to aid them in their efforts. We ask them to repeat information (through verbal or written means), sometimes without them analyzing or even comprehending it. If the child can perform this recitation, the adult feels confident that this child has met certain goals that are explicitly known by the adult alone.

But isn't true knowing more than that? Isn't the way we adapt our thoughts according to our own experiences, and how we apply new knowledge to different experiences, a much better barometer of the evidence of real learning? Sometimes, we need to encounter something many times and see it in many ways before we can incorporate it into our thinking. What if we allowed children to sit with ideas for longer than a day or a week? What if we encouraged them to communicate what they knew through expressive modalities that came naturally to them? What if we allowed them the time to apply their knowledge to new contexts and problems? That's the power of self-directed learning.

Discovering Interests

I often hear from parents that one of their biggest concerns is that they'll carve out intentional time in the day for independent pursuits and their children will do nothing with it. Some children easily divulge their interests, plans, and questions; others don't. Parents of the latter may worry that their children will reveal "subpar" interests—or that they don't have any interests and passions at all.

In her book *Project-Based Homeschooling*, Lori Pickert writes:

> The importance of a child's authentic interest cannot be overemphasized. Without it, learning is like pushing a boulder uphill. With it, we're pushing the boulder downhill. Learning occurs in both directions. So why do we usually go with the uphill option? It boils down to fear. Or, nervousness. Nervousness that a child won't get all the important knowledge that he needs (radius of Mars, exports of Peru). Nervousness that a child who is allowed to pursue his own interests won't learn the important lessons of how to buckle down and do work that is boring, uninteresting, and meaningless.[3]

On the surface, it's easy to understand how a child's interests are important. But what are we to make of them? How do we help our children to determine their interests with the hope that they'll be motivated to do something with them?

First, as I mentioned before, we must realize that children develop the ability to stay with an interest longer over time. When your children are young, sustained interest might look different than it will five years from now. Often, we are looking for our children to run with a "deep interest" or passion and know immediately from the start in what direction they should be headed. Instead, we should probably be encouraging them to have new experiences, play, tinker, experiment, and explore new materials, especially when there are lulls between their moments of taking initiative. The deep interest will come, but it can't be forced. Sometimes you must get started in what might look like surface-level investigation and let opportunities for engagement come naturally.

For children who may be unsure of what might draw their attention for any length of time, we must consider some of the things that actually reveal their interests:

- How they spend their free time
- What they play with and the choices they make in their play
- Their questions
- Their conversations
- The books they read
- The things they watch or the content they consume
- Their plans

For children who reveal interests that we have no desire to support because we think that they're not academic enough or interesting enough, we must remember this: It's not about the topic or project; it's about the skills learned along the way. When my children go in a direction that I wouldn't have chosen or explore a topic that I don't particularly love, I must remind myself whose work it is in the first place. Then I must do my own work of dealing with my discomfort so that they're free to do theirs. When it's hard for me to see value in something they find interesting, I need to intentionally find something about the process that I *can* support. Research, communicating information to others (artistically, verbally, and through writing), making plans, documenting results, managing a club, comparing information, experimenting, making a draft, overcoming a difficulty, working through a mistake . . . those can all be parts of the process of building knowledge when we endeavor to find out more about something. I get behind their efforts and try not to pay as much attention to the topic.

At the same time, I make a mental note to investigate more deeply. I get curious about what it is they're doing and what value it holds for them. I initiate conversations that will help me understand what purpose they'd like their work to serve. I'm usually surprised by the things I learn in those interactions. When I was uncomfortable with one child's seeming obsession with a video game, I leaned in and started to ask more questions. What resulted was a phenomenon I have noticed time and time again: There comes a point when they begin to want to generate or create the things they've been assimilating through their own experiences. That conversation with my child led to the start of coding classes when I finally understood what he wanted to do. Relatedly, when I handed this same child a camera and asked him to take screenshots of challenges, victories, or worlds in his game, and then interviewed him to learn more about the photos, I was subtly helping him to document his work and reflect on his process. After realizing that he needed help to beat a certain level, I supported him through his efforts to research and find useful tips.

Video Games and Screen Time

Uh oh. Do you sense that proverbial can of worms that has just been opened? Usually, if I mention video games and Project Time together, those worms come crawling out with ferocity. So let's deal with them. Allow me to interrupt this discourse on discovering interests to tackle a common fear: *If I structure our days around interest-led learning and give my children freedom to choose how they spend their time, they'll just want to play video games or be glued to a screen all day.*

Beyond my one example above, I want to tell you about some ways we have handled this. I also want to tell you how I've coached parents to approach the same concerns when I am consulting with them about project-based learning. So, if that nagging fear comes true, this section will give you some options to consider.

If you find these suggestions confusing or contradictory, take a deep, slow, cleansing breath. You're in the right place. Consider this section permission not to have the perfect response to one of your biggest fears already figured out. You have the freedom to accept the layers of nuance that will exist for every interest or passion your child has, alongside your family values, your feelings, your biases, and your developing understanding. There's no one perfect way to do this kind of work in your home. But don't let your questions or your uncertainty be a barrier to getting started or doing more interest-led learning. Keep the inner dialogue going. Keep asking yourself why you're making the choices you're making. Keep trying to understand the work your children are doing, and you'll find that it becomes a journey of growth for everyone involved.

Do Nothing

Gasp! Yes, it's true—doing nothing is one of your options. You can choose not to fight or question your child's interest in video games, but rather to let it play out and see where it leads, staying open to discovery and adjustments along the way. It might be helpful to think through what your initial response will be. Are there ground rules that everyone must agree on? Are you willing to make it a free-for-all at first to get a sense of what your child really wants to do or play?

We can all admit to some degree that not all video games are bad. In fact, there's even research indicating the benefits of video game play when balanced with other pursuits. In an *American Psychologist* article, researchers write that "taken together, these findings suggest that video games provide youth with immersive and compelling social, cognitive, and emotional experiences. Further, these experiences may have the potential to enhance mental health and well-being in children and adolescents" by, for example, "having them work toward meaningful goals, persevere in the face of multiple failures, and celebrate the rare moments of triumph after successfully completing challenging tasks."[4]

Maybe you're skeptical of this research. Maybe you're thinking, *Okay, but just because video games* can *be beneficial doesn't mean they necessarily* will *be*. Perhaps your uneasy feelings about the entire topic will remain even after choosing this option. However, your openness to learn and understand will serve everyone well. There is no flawless path to attempting Project Time or incorporating gaming as an interest or self-directed pursuit. You must only remain willing to take the journey.

Operate from Abundance, Not Scarcity

Parents often feel that their children "play video games too much" or "are addicted to screens" because they're operating on what psychologists call the scarcity principle, which says that we tend to value something more when it is in short supply. They feel that other things they also value (reading good books, spending time outdoors, playing a musical instrument) are happening infrequently by comparison. So the antidote to excessive screen time might be to actually spend time, and a healthy portion of it, on things you highly value. If your child is dedicating many hours to video game play, then choose a different interest of theirs to support. You won't be as eager to control whatever remaining "free time" your child spends on games if you're satisfied by the rebalance of time.

Your child might also be operating on their own scarcity principle, coveting video game play because it seems rare. Project-based homeschooling guru Lori Pickert emphasizes a balance between doing the things that are meaningful for the family while also allowing for "generous limits" on game time that don't make your children feel shortchanged or devalued. She writes, "Screens were fun, but the kids never riveted on them because there was no need to. If they wanted to get to level 47 of some game, they had plenty of time to do that. Employing generous limits means you have plenty of time. You don't worry—there's no urgency. You aren't hyper-focused on it, and your mind is free to focus on and enjoy other things. And we made sure they had plenty of other things to focus on."[5]

When time seems abundant, you can put more effort into helping your older children learn to manage their time independently by teaching them how to be balanced. My daughter, for example, loves to dedicate hours to her art. She'll sit at her desk for long stretches, sculpting something from clay or painting details on what she's sculpted. She also loves gaming with friends and could easily do that for hours as well, but if you ask her if she'd trade her art time for video game time, she'll say no. (I'm not assuming—I've asked!) Because of the space she has in her day, she has discovered pleasures she wants to dedicate time to. When other activities and interests emerge, she must employ time management skills to ultimately do everything she wants to do and be happy. Those are skills that grow over time and don't magically get figured out overnight—many adults struggle with them too!—but we can begin to support their development through this kind of work.

Base Projects on Games

Challenge your child to take their interest in video games and do projects about it during times not dedicated to gameplay. For instance, they might want to focus on some complexities of the game, like the development of worlds, character design, puzzle solving, and so on. Or they might want to explore related experiences like making tip videos on how to conquer a level or a podcast on the features of various games. When my son wanted to figure out how to write code and create a game, he used Project Time to develop the story and the characters. Projects like these take their interest a little further and a little deeper.

Some children will take you up on this offer if they get the sense that you're not trying to trick or manipulate them, while other children will feel like you are trying to "schoolify" something they find pleasurable. A lot of this comes down to the relationship between the two of you. Are you making demands and asserting parental power, or are you demonstrating curiosity, authentically conversing, honestly communicating your own questions and fears, and negotiating a result that everyone can live with? If that seems impossible, abort and find some other interest to support.

Discuss the Why

Consider the *why* behind your children's consumption of video games and screen time. Take a step back and do the work—together with your children—to let these things exist healthily in your home. For a while, my daughter spent large amounts of her Project Time watching dog training videos. I didn't have a problem with what she was watching, but when I glanced over at her in front of a *screen*, watching video after video, I just had an uneasy feeling. She noticed my uncomfortable body language, and we talked about it. She told me the *why* behind her desire to watch the videos and the bigger purpose she wanted them to serve: She wanted to diversify her dog training sources and see how it might influence her work with our family dog, which was an ongoing interest that began years prior with visiting that service dog facility. She was connecting it all.

In this and many other instances, my children and I have conversations about what makes the content we consume on a screen worth the time we invest in it, whether we can sort or classify types of content based on the feelings they produce or the purposes they serve, and why it matters. We do this because we want to be able to make balanced decisions about the space we allow screens and online media to occupy in our schedules and daily routines. As I write this book, my children see me in front of a screen for hours and hours at a time. They would have no idea why I'm making this choice with my time if I didn't talk to them about what I'm doing and what my goals are.

In the end, analytical discussion and engaged collaboration around video games and screen time (or any issues that might cause contention) will hopefully lead to thoughtful, intentional, and principled choices about what and how to consume or create content of similar kinds, now and throughout life.

Ebb and Flow

When I have a new interest or there's something I want to learn, I'm usually really excited about it at first. I'll stay up late to research or find time to experiment and play. I'll think about it constantly. Then, somewhere along the way, my enthusiasm might wane, simply because there are days when I'm tired, I have more pressing things to do, or I'm in search of some new inspiration. But the interest is still there. Time is somewhat irrelevant. What matters is that my desire to learn something (whatever it is) has remained, even though I might be frustrated by my slow progress, my inability to focus solely on that thing, or some other challenges. I would say that's pretty normal behavior, wouldn't you?

Yet sometimes we expect that our children will choose a project or something to explore and will want to work on it every. Single. Day. When we're learning, there are ebbs and flows, starts and stops that are part of a natural process and pace. Even passions aren't pursued passionately 100 percent of the time. They're developed over time by learning and practicing the skills that support them.

My children once became interested in paper planes and worked on them off and on. Some days they were outside, testing out planes they made. On other days, they were inside devouring books about paper planes. One child got especially interested in pictures that showed how to fold planes in ways that affected things like lift, drag, thrust, and weight. After making and testing about twenty planes, they asked for help creating a large chart to compare and contrast all of them. But it wasn't every day. After a week or two went by, one might even think that they were no longer interested. But then they'd be back, informally interviewing people about their favorite paper planes, watching countless how-to videos, and playing with their planes.

I found myself evaluating the meaning of "sustained interest." I realized that although at times it means that something captures our attention for a long block of time (and that is a wonderful thing to find), it can also mean that we've found something appealing enough to abide within the natural rhythm of passing time. It's easy for us as parents to withhold our support until we see evidence of "real interest," but when we join our children in their journey to discover anything new, we're sending the message that their ideas are worth chasing.

This work is best understood by taking ourselves through the same learning, discovery, and experimentation processes; asking ourselves the same questions; and observing our own feelings, decisions, frustrations, and methods as we become the learners, workers, and doers. It's easy to forget all these things if we're solely focused on our children and our desire for them to develop into competent learners who are passionate about their work. We forget that it's about the process, and we forget that process altogether if we're not engaged in it ourselves.

A Mentoring Relationship

Another way you can help develop the interests you observe in your children is to assume the role of a mentor. Have you ever had a mentor? If the answer is yes, then you could probably make a list of all the benefits of having one. I've had mentors, and here are some benefits I've noticed:

- It's a long-term, real relationship.
- There is mutual respect and trust.
- They support your growth.
- They provide encouragement, feedback, and advice.
- They help you solve problems without taking over.
- They are focused on your development.

This short list helps me understand how I want to mentor my children through their learning, endeavors, pursuits, and projects.

How would you define a mentor's role? The Alliance for Self-Directed Education has this to say: "Being self-directed doesn't mean going it alone. Aside from modeling by pursuing their own growth and learning, caretakers and other adults *facilitate* Self-Directed Education by providing access to resources, creating SDE-friendly environments, and engaging in authentic conversations prompted by the learners' curiosities."[6]

We're mentoring our children to become learners and workers who can manage and direct their own work, which means that we're also guiding them toward independence. We're supporting without controlling, inviting their voices and ideas into the process wherever and however we can. That means affirming their ability to do things like find information, choose their resources, sort out their finds, compare their sources, and throw out what doesn't work. These are important skills that will carry over to anything they attempt to learn, so we want to reinforce them.

When our children do what they want to do in a meaningful way it will have a combination of effects, like gaining insight into work they might choose for the next time, developing self-awareness and refining their thought process, learning better ways of researching, and experiencing all-around growth. It's not about the work they choose; it's about the learners they become. Over time, we can also get better at mentoring them along the way.

Sometimes our role as a mentor is to ask questions—the kinds of questions that help our children realize what their own questions are and seek solutions, or that help drive their work forward. There are times that our questions will promote just the right amount of "disequilibrium" to help them see from a new perspective. I like to ask questions like, *What are your plans? How did you decide that you were finished with this? What's next? How could you find out? What other ways do you think this topic can be explored? Is it possible to investigate this by working with your hands? Are there other ways? What has been challenging for you and why? What do you notice?*

Ultimately, I think that the mentoring role is to validate, trust, and support the ways that children create knowledge. Loris Malaguzzi, the founder of the Reggio Emilia Approach to education, has a famous poem about the "hundred languages" of children, which is to say, the multiplicity of ways children formulate, express, and connect their ideas.[7] This is true whether the child is three or thirteen. To help our children toward in-depth inquiry and exploration of meaningful ideas, we need to carefully observe their "hundred languages" process— pay attention to it, make time for it, consistently validate it, celebrate it, and talk about it like the high level of learning that it is.

In order to do that, we must first examine our own biases and ask ourselves whether we trust the learning process. When children explore things in a hands-on way, do we assume that they're learning or not learning? Do we believe that they're capable of both figuring things out and bringing fresh ideas to the table? How many times have you witnessed your child immersed in something in ways that demonstrated deep interest but thought, *Okay, now that's enough, because we have to get to the next subject?* An example: I mentioned earlier how my daughter spends an endless amount of time engaged in her art. If you're an artist, you know that it's easy to devote *many* hours in the day to the practice of your passion, but I think many parents of child artists struggle with exactly *how* much time we're talking about here and whether it counts as "learning."

If you can become even a little bit curious about what might happen if you turned over to your child the ability to navigate how they spend their time, it just might be enough motivation to try and find out. Maybe you'll be pleasantly surprised. Maybe you'll discover something you didn't know before. Perhaps you'll realize that it's possible with parameters. You'll work together to figure out all the other stuff you're worried is *not* getting done. Our children need time to dedicate to passionate pursuits. They will lead us. They will show us what they need. Their needs will change as projects, interests, and maturity levels change, but they will always need our trust, our support, and our mentorship.

We need to remember that the self-directed work that a child does and the learning that happens around it are not rigid experiences that have a defined beginning, middle, or end. We often want our children to produce something that culminates their research and makes *us* feel good about our efforts to *let* them learn this way. But what if the work has multiple beginnings? What if it unfolds organically or develops intuitively, sometimes without a plan? What if it repeats and spirals and has many intricate layers? This is about letting go—a relinquishment of control on our part and an embrace of a slower pace that allows for true inquiry-based learning. What better place is there to do that than right at home?

In sum, we mentor by helping our children to go deeper. That means we encourage better understanding and insight. We support immersion and more attentive involvement. We model attention to detail and discernment of nuances. We invite independence and more genuine experiences. We reflect their own awareness. We mirror enthusiasm and appreciate honest work. Some interpret all this to mean that we somehow put "academic" demands on something our children want to do for fun, but that isn't the case at all. It is our intention to *support* that matters. We can't predicate what support should look like in a way that doesn't consider the individuality of each child and the work they take on.

Again, there's no perfect way to begin the process. We adjust, grow, and get better along the way. Here are some questions to help you think about how you can cultivate this approach daily:

- What is necessary for natural learning to occur? What is needed on a very basic level?

- What is required of you, of your children, of your home?

- Does your home environment allow opportunities to pursue personal interests? How? How can it be improved?

- What home routines would support self-directed learning?

- What is your role? What does a good mentor do?

- How can you recognize the evidence of learning even without visual or physical work? (More on this in chapter 8.)

- What is a good starting place to implement this way of learning? (Hint: It doesn't have to be all or nothing, or the only thing that you do.)

Let me be clear: Self-directed learning will happen in some way, whether we embrace it or not, because it is a very natural process for discovering just about anything. If you pay attention, you'll see evidence of it. But the degree to which you celebrate, support, and make time for it in your home is where the "embrace" aspect comes in. Some families are doing nothing but self-directed learning, while others are doing it along with other types of study or curriculum. I'll say again that it doesn't have to be all or nothing.

Observing and Nurturing Strengths

In a piece I wrote for the homeschool community Wild + Free, I argued that, often without even meaning to, we look at children's learning through a model that focuses on their deficits, or what they can't do, rather than their competencies, or what they can do.[8] The deficiencies seem to be glaring at us, taunting us, guilting us into getting "serious" so we can drill them away. As a result, we see our role as one of directing and sometimes coercing rather than one of partnership and trust. Yet, as educator Patricia Carini wrote, "each of us is . . . a complex blend of failings and virtues, of strengths and vulnerabilities."[9] If we're going to go slow and go deep, we might as well invest the time necessary to see our children through a model that focuses less on their deficits and more on their competencies.

How do we identify those competencies? By observing our children's passions. For children and adults alike, passions reveal areas of strength. Abiding interests can give us insight into how people connect ideas and acquire knowledge. They also develop in such a way that over time, they strengthen habits of mind, grow solid skills, and can even become lifelong pleasures. Carini wrote that children's strengths are

> observable wherever the learning environment provides the child with the opportunity to make choices and state preferences . . . and the opportunity to contribute ideas and raise questions that will be heard and responded to . . . To see the child from a variety of perspectives, in different contexts, engaged with varied materials, and most importantly, *through time* is the key to observations. . . . The other side of observation is remembering and reflecting.[10]

In other words, when we repeatedly observe our children engaging with their interests in natural ways, we notice things we might not notice if we didn't see them engaged in a wide variety of self-directed pursuits. This gives us valuable information about their strengths that we can then commit to nurturing. To nurture these strengths is to continue to make room for them to be practiced without interference, to draw on them as we engage our children in other areas, and to hold space for them while honoring the complexity and ever-changing nature of who our children are becoming.

We must help create the context for strengths to be seen, and we must expect that our children will apply them broadly. As we allow their strengths to inform our understanding of them as growing learners, we will love and guide them with a heart that sees beyond their struggles and knows their capacity. It matters.

Loose Parts

As you consider your child's interests and how to explore them, let's talk practically for a moment about materials. I've always seen the value in having open-ended materials around to help support my children in their efforts of making and doing. I anticipate that they'll want ample time to investigate them, and I keep an open mind about where they could lead. In many early-childhood educational circles, these open-ended materials are referred to as "loose parts." In a nutshell, loose parts are materials without a predetermined purpose. Children can make their own choices about how they would like to use them.

Sometimes it is from these materials that interests emerge and extend. They have been the raw materials my children have needed to help them develop skills while exploring a topic more deeply. For example, my son worked with Lego bricks for a long time before he felt comfortable using them to come up with his own builds. He needed to try them out at his leisure before he was confident about what they could do. Eventually, while creating more intricate things, he also began to explore adjacent interests like model-making of complicated functions, simple machines, and engineering. Similarly, when my children wanted to make a representation of the Rosetta stone, they came back to something familiar: They chose to use a type of clay that they had worked with before, because they were confident in their knowledge of how to use it to prepare and cut slabs.

When I was an elementary school teacher, I worked in a particular school that had a dedicated project room just for the upper grades. It was quite a sight to behold. A woodworking table sat in the middle of the room. To one side, there was a makeshift kitchen in which students would daily prepare snacks like bacalaitos and oatmeal cookies; to the other side, an area where children would create the most spectacular block constructions and marble runs. There was generous table space peppered throughout the room, and the walls were lined with bins upon bins of materials or loose parts. The children used the materials to do things like creating games with unique game pieces, building replicas and scale models of various spaces, designing skateboards with an interesting assortment of parts, and making basic mechanical devices. Open-ended materials lend themselves to a diverse set of users, regardless of age.

Here are some examples of useful loose parts:

- **Nature-based:** pine cones, leaves, dried flowers, sand, wood cookies, acorns, sticks, feathers, shells, cinnamon sticks, rocks, geodes, etc.

- **Metal:** foil, nuts and bolts, washers, metal lids, old keys, soda can tabs, forks and spoons, cans, etc.

- **Wood:** clothespins, wood scraps, wood frames, dowels, pegs, corks, spools, skewers, toothpicks, craft sticks, etc.

- **Ceramic and glass:** tiles, glass beads, marbles, sea glass, tiny bottles and containers, gems, mirrors, etc.

- **Plastic:** funnels, food containers, bottle caps, marker caps, cups, straws, bottles, PVC piping, etc.

- **Packaging/cardboard:** bubble wrap, boxes, cardboard scraps, paper towel and toilet paper rolls, egg cartons, cereal boxes, wrapping paper, packing peanuts, etc.

- **Fabric/yarn/ribbon:** burlap, rope, ribbon, twine, string, felt squares, fabric scraps, chiffon scarves, yarn, embroidery floss, wool, lace, etc.

I'm not saying to go out and find everything on the list. Just start small and simple. What's around your home already that you don't need to go out and buy? It's not about having everything, just considering what's available to you right now. Additionally, basic supplies like colored pencils, crayons, markers, paper, tape, scissors, and so on are all great to have on hand.

One question to ask is, "What might you be able to do with this?" Such a simple question, right? But it can be a powerful one in encouraging creative thinking and exploration. Once I gave some old pulleys to a group of children, posing this same question. I was impressed with their willingness to experiment. I also like to show my children photos of interesting things others have done with random materials and parts for inspiration.

Sometimes it's hard to imagine what a child could accomplish with materials that don't have a predetermined purpose. People wonder what the benefit is of giving children loose parts to play with. But think of how creative and experimental one must be to assign one's own meaning to an object. We've all heard parents quip about how their children have more interest in the box a gift came in than in the actual gift itself, haven't we? Children crave these types of imaginative, expressive experiences. Their natural inclination is toward exploration and wonder.

If you decide to offer open-ended materials in your home and your child doesn't magically begin to use them in the ways that you've imagined, don't let that derail you. There are so many possibilities for use in self-directed pursuits, but ideas take time. Remember that sometimes we need to sit with a material long enough to be confident about what that material can do. It is only with this confidence that we move forward into more profound pursuits.

This is true for younger children and also older children who, in addition to loose parts, might be using a wider variety of materials. Older children can be very helpful in coming up with a list of supplies that are open-ended enough to invite exploration and also useful for things they're trying to accomplish. In fact, when I surveyed my older children and asked them about the supplies they liked to have on hand while pursuing their various interests, they came up with the following (for brevity, I've eliminated anything that was already on the list above):

- **Paints and paint supplies:** quality brushes, watercolors, gouache, acrylic paint, puffy paint, spray paint, assorted painting paper, canvases, paint trays, easel

- **Clay/modeling materials:** polymer clay, air-dry clay, terracotta oven-bake clay, Apoxie Sculpt, pottery plaster, clay tools and cutters, pottery wheel

- **Other art supplies:** gel pens, regular pens, various lead pencils, blending stumps, erasers, alcohol ink, sketchbooks, watercolor pencils, oil pastels, beeswax crayons

- **Paper:** computer paper, sketch paper, white tissue paper, card stock, parchment paper, music staff paper, kite paper, origami paper, solar print paper, scratch paper, cotton rag paper

- **Sewing, needlework, and textile supplies:** needles, thread, embroidery hoops, crochet hooks, knitting needles, weaving loom, wool for needle felting, felting tools, stuffing, elastic

- **Miscellaneous craft and experimenting supplies:** hot glue, regular glue, super glue, scissors, hole punch, craft foam, Q-tips, cotton balls, fishing line, artificial sinew, food coloring, wire, rubber bands, paper clips, balloons, stamps, flower press, empty containers, test tubes, droppers, plant pots, soil, kinetic sand, buttons, pipe cleaners, tea lights, cigar boxes, jewelry-making supplies

- **Tools and hardware:** pliers, batteries, copper wire, light bulbs, electronic buzzers, springs, wire cutters, wood tools, nails, carving knives/whittling kit, neodymium magnets, magnetic tape, flashlight, magnifying glass, pulleys, soldering iron, rotary tool, small motors, power tools

- **Construction toys:** Lego, K'Nex, standard unit wood blocks

- **Equipment:** podcast mic, webcam, GoPro, voice recorder, camera, studio lighting, paper cutter, sewing machine, Cricut, laminator, printer, digital microscope, balance scale, digital drawing pad and pen, drone, robotics kit, computer

(Side note: My children are never shy about asking neighbors, family, and friends to borrow or help them use equipment that we don't personally own.)

This is all in addition to books and guides on a range of topics, including calligraphy, music composition, sewing, macramé, puppet making, wood carving, finger knitting, physics experiments, electric gadgets, entrepreneurship, cardboard toys, paper miniatures, paper engineering, building and construction, comic creation, corrugated cardboard creations, kites, terrariums, and dollhouses.

I have also been known to leave interesting books, photos, and materials lying around for my children to discover and hopefully find inspiration from (a practice known as "strewing" in the unschooling community). Handmade toys, paper airplanes, bridges, graffiti art, recipes, fiber art . . . virtually anything can encourage new thoughts and ideas.

Tips for Project Time

My number-one tip for getting started with Project Time is simply to make time for engaging in personal interests and meaningful pursuits. It doesn't even have to look like a dedicated block of time, as it does in my home. That is how we flow best, but truth be told, deep, abiding interests bleed out into other parts of the day and weekends too.

Project Time for you could mean that your children are already dedicating themselves to their passions and you're simply there for authentic conversation. Relationship and your genuine curiosity about what they are doing or studying will help you avoid the impulse to usurp control. (Remember the video games can of worms?) In addition, your role might be to support the potential for connections to related experiences at times when your child is not engaged in their personal work. For example, when my daughter was interested in birds, I made a point of visiting the local center for birds of prey. I knew it would be a great way for her to expand her knowledge. You could also relay to them your own observations of their work and create opportunities to honor that work. Look for ways to make them feel like their work is important no matter the topic.

You might need to build up to self-directed learning in small ways. Some children need something more than, "Here's a Project Time! Now, go make it great!" Perhaps it would be better to start by giving them more choice and control over things you are already doing. Get their feedback and ask for input before you make all the decisions. Invite them to design small parts of their day.

Project Time Ideas

If you want some ideas to help you get started, here's a list of some of the projects my children have done during Project Time. I don't mean to give the impression that these projects should be prescriptively re-created, or that your children are doing something wrong if they're not doing projects like these, but I know that having some examples can help people visualize and understand what is possible, especially if they've never attempted Project Time before. Remember that all self-directed work begins with the interests of *your* children. On any given day, at any given age or stage of development, these interests could change and look completely different. As you'll see from these examples, Project Time invites children to build, create, and do—and to bring their penchant for play into the process.

BOARD GAME CREATION

One child created a board game. He invented and wrote out the rules, aiming for the appropriate level of challenge. He also designed and constructed the game board, game pieces, and other components. When he was satisfied that it was ready for use, he invited others to play.

BOOK WRITING/ILLUSTRATION

My son wrote a story that was modeled after the Beatrix Potter tales. He noticed that her illustrations were made with ink and watercolor, so he did the same. A couple years later, he repeated this process with a longer story and self-published his work.

BOW AND ARROW

My son wanted to create his own bow and arrows using wood, sinew, and arrowheads. He researched mostly Powhatan techniques and tried to learn as much as he could. The work itself involved a lot of trial and error. We found artificial sinew, and he was able to create a functional bow. However, it was difficult for him to find the appropriate amount of tension that would send the arrow flying as far as he wanted it to. He concluded his work by writing up things he was learning in his research.

CHESS

Occasionally, someone dedicates their Project Time to playing chess. They practice strategies and have even taught others to play. Although they've taken a class here and there, they prefer to work on their game through discovery, practice, and play with more advanced players.

DRAWING

Sometimes my children sketch freely in a sketchbook, and at other times they draw specific characters or subjects, in which case they draw along with a tutorial. Projects like these usually run for days until interest wears thin or they're just ready to move on to something new. It's something that they revisit again and again.

ELECTRICITY AND ELECTRICAL ENGINEERING

One son got interested in electricity after seeing his brother explore circuits for weeks. He started playing with copper wires, batteries, and bulbs the same way he saw his brother doing and started to make some of the same discoveries. He drew pictures of the circuits that he tried and asked me to help him make notes about what did and didn't work. By this point, his older brother had enrolled in a self-paced online electrical engineering class, where he learned to make more complicated circuits on a grid using resistors.

JEWELRY MAKING AND SELLING

My daughter creates different types of jewelry, crafted from a wide variety of materials. She sells her jewelry as well, so she's had to learn to manage her sales, organize her inventory, restock supplies, and keep track of her expenses. This project inspired her to also open a bank account and budget her money.

KINETIC SAND

This was a daily obsession in our home for a very long time. I had huge plastic bins filled with kinetic sand in which my children would create Jurassic worlds, historical dioramas, neighborhoods, race car tracks, volcanoes and other geographical features, and archaeology dig sites. They also used molds and tools for creating patterns and designs in the sand. All of these included elements of pretend play.

LITERARY COOKING

My children researched and re-created recipes from literature like *Midsummer's Mayhem* by Rajani LaRocca, *Redwall* by Brian Jacques, and *Pie* by Sarah Weeks. Choosing stories, collecting recipes, sorting through them, making ingredient lists, shopping, planning, and preparing were also part of the process. This interest spanned over a few months.

MAPMAKING

My son was playing with superhero figures and kept making them fly around the world during imaginative play. He pulled his brothers into the scene, all of them looking at the globe and trying to name where they were flying. They questioned where things were and how far these places were from home. I simply observed and recorded their questions and then one day pointed out to them what I had noticed. It was enough for one child to realize he wanted answers to some of his questions. For the next few weeks, he read about places that interested him, made multiple 2D and 3D representations of world maps, and noted down facts he deemed worthy of recording.

MORSE CODE, CIPHERS, CODES, AND PUZZLES

This was a fun exploration that invited the participation of family members willing to solve or search for clues along the way. Inspired by Jennifer Chambliss Bertman's *Book Scavenger*, they mailed letters with hidden messages to friends and even hid ciphers in public for people to find.

OBSTACLE COURSE

Some of my children created an obstacle course for a pet guinea pig. They collaborated on a design and used various loose parts to construct it, refining their process as they went along. It involved stopping a lot to play and experiment with the guinea pig.

KNIGHTS AND SWORDS

After reading books and watching movies set during medieval times, my children had a growing interest in knights and swords. They designed and crafted swords from a variety of materials like cardboard, foam core, and wood. They also designed and sewed clothing that they used for armor and outer garments. The things they created went through many revisions as they tried to figure out ways to reinforce the structure of the weapons, fit clothing to the right size, and accommodate their changing design details.

PEG DOLL CHARACTERS

For a while, a few of my children loved to paint peg dolls, mostly choosing characters from the chapter books we read together as a family, with interest resurfacing at the start of every new story. They used acrylic paint and very thin brushes for fine details, which was a challenge in dexterity. They also loved playing with the characters they created.

PUBLIC SPEAKING

My son became fascinated with the art of communicating effectively in front of an audience of people. He decided to study people he enjoyed listening to and tried to figure out what made them good at what they did. He also tried to develop his own ability to speak publicly.

READING

If a child has a goal to finish a particular book or even a series that includes quite a few books, he or she will often dedicate large amounts of time, including Project Times, to reading. They usually find a cozy corner of the house to get comfortable and disappear inside the pages of a book.

SIGN LANGUAGE

One child decided to dedicate time to learning American Sign Language. He enjoys being self-taught but has expressed interest in taking a formal class. He started to research different possibilities for this but also has other interests demanding his attention, so it hasn't progressed beyond this point for now.

SILENT FILM

After reading *The Nerviest Girl in the World* by Melissa Wiley, my children decided they wanted to make a silent film. That took over Project Time for a while. They researched and then got to work making costumes and props. They wrote a script, conducted rehearsals, and recorded and edited the film. They worked together and divvied up responsibilities and roles according to everyone's strengths and interests.

STORY PROJECTIONS

I had one of those old overhead projectors lying around, so we set it up opposite a blank wall. My children used clear transparencies to draw scenes from stories, which they then projected onto the wall. They ended up presenting their work as a show.

TOY CUSTOMIZATION

My daughter has had a long-time interest in customizing Littlest Pet Shop toys. She paints blank molds of the figures in unique ways and sculpts pieces to add to the figures. She has had to experiment with different types of materials for sculpting and become more and more knowledgeable about each one. She sells her custom figures and has had to figure out an online platform to best accomplish that. She has also produced scripted videos using the figures as characters, as well as videos demonstrating her clay and painting techniques.

TREE STUDY

This began with a series of questions about knots, rings, and tree nutrition that I jotted down in a note on my phone as my children asked them. I then reminded my son about the questions later. He started by researching and reading as much as he could find and investigated trees right in our yard and neighborhood.

WOODWORKING

Different children at different times have worked with tools to build various items like a birdhouse, a bird feeder, pencil holders, and toy swords. They also enjoy shadowing their dad if he's building something larger, like furniture. In the process, they learn about power tools and different elements of design and construction. These same children also enjoy whittling wood into various objects.

CHAPTER 7

Learning at a Different Tempo

Surprise, Flexibility, and Spontaneity

*The paradox is that Slow does not always mean slow.
As we shall see, performing a task in a Slow manner often yields
faster results. It is also possible to do things quickly while
maintaining a Slow frame of mind.*

—CARL HONORÉ, *IN PRAISE OF SLOWNESS*

This chapter will provide practical help for parents who want to broadly apply the principles of slow schooling to all areas of learning. We will look at three elements that I think are key when interacting with a host of topics, especially when we're in control of our pace: surprise, flexibility, and spontaneity. These can be woven into learning in a way that safeguards our internal sense of "slow." The examples you'll read throughout this chapter will hopefully help spark your own ideas of ways of weaving these three elements into learning. This is neither a comprehensive catalog of activities nor a thorough exposition of ways of experimenting with education's tempo. However, it is an ardent invitation to widen your view of how learning can be experienced. So let's explore these three elements a bit further.

Surprise

When my children were younger, they watched a video of scientist Cheryl Hayashi discussing her amazing work with spider silk. One of my sons kept shaking his head and saying that he didn't even know people did that kind of research or that it could be someone's job. His sense of surprise at this new information inspired in him an unexpected fascination with spiders, and his interest began to influence the rest of the family. We searched for different kinds of spiderwebs out in the wild. We tried to identify various spiders by their distinguishing features while walking around the neighborhood. We watched spiny orb weavers methodically spin their webs right outside of our front door. We even watched a golden silk spider capture and eat its prey. I think we were all a little surprised by just how far our fascination carried us.

Surprise is what we feel when we encounter something new, awesome, delightful, or unplanned. Becoming someone who embraces and incorporates surprise into learning involves a blend of different factors, including making time for the things that cause it. In their book *Surprise*, researchers Tania Luna and LeeAnn Renninger show how "individuals who are skilled in embracing the unpredictable and engineering the unexpected"[1] are uniquely equipped to thrive in life. Those who welcome and harness surprise do these three things well: "build resilience, reframe vulnerability, and practice skillful not-knowing."[2]

Our children will respond well to surprise when they have:

- Security and support in an educational atmosphere where values are clear (chapter 3).

- A safe place to be vulnerable, without fear that their every move will be evaluated negatively by the adults around them (chapter 4).

- Stability in the presence of routines that they can trust (chapter 5).

And when we, as parents have:

- Considered what is negatively dominating the homeschool experience so that we can work on reframing it (chapter 2). Is it tears every time you ask a child to write? Failure to understand or learn multiplication? Tension about the best way to tackle high school science? Reframing helps us to ponder what these experiences are teaching us and get closer to what we really want.

- Set attainable goals and helped our children to experience success before asking them to do something much more difficult (chapter 8).

- Invited flexibility into the home (more on that later in this chapter).

Using these ideas as a framework for how the element of surprise can vary the way we experience time while learning, let's focus on wonder. Wonder is often the trigger for the surprise and admiration we feel when we encounter something new, awesome, delightful, or unplanned. I like to think of seeking wonder as taking time to marvel and be amazed. The simple act of wondering about something can often open the door to a host of other opportunities.

Manoush Zomorodi, in a chapter called "Reclaiming Wonder" from her book *Bored and Brilliant*, encourages readers to "observe something else"[3] as one of the challenges in a series designed to help people forget their devices in favor of letting their minds wander and unlocking creativity. In this particular challenge, which involves an "energetic fascination with the world"[4] around you, she tells the story of an art student Nisha, who accepted the Bored and Brilliant challenge and one day noticed details about a postcard that had been hanging on her wall for years. It led her to research the artist who created it, his artistic techniques, and the story behind his work. She even attempted to produce her own art in a similar style. Reflecting on this participant's experience, Zomorodi writes, "Nisha's story encapsulates everything that Bored and Brilliant is supposed to be about: letting your mind wander wherever it wants to go; seeing old things in a new way; making new connections; taking micro risks; and surprising yourself."[5]

Building in surprise and wonder is a matter of honing your attention and being primed for whatever comes next. So how else can we encourage our children to see more sharply and regard everyone and everything surrounding them more richly? How can we help them hone their attention and direct them toward the possibility of surprise? Here are a few ways.

Planning for Pauses

Planning for pauses is looking at what you're studying and planning out the places where you'll stop and linger, leaving room for surprise and wonder. It can be done with just about anything you're studying.

For example, when my family made our first foray into the world of Shakespeare, we began with Leon Garfield's *Shakespeare Stories*, which is written in a way that preserves the richness of Shakespeare's language yet is accessible to a younger audience. I found a local public theater that would be featuring a free performance of one of the plays, and I planned our timing so that we'd read only a few stories in the collection before we attended. Essentially, the performance gave us a pause to experience the play differently and open ourselves up to whatever surprises we might encounter. I arranged that pause in advance, and we adjusted ourselves accordingly, abandoning our regular routine to do something that would allow us to learn more about the topic at hand. We did the same thing with a free performance of Handel's *Messiah* when studying the oratorio and with a museum exhibit when reading about mummification around the world.

But these opportunities don't always come from theaters, performances, or museums. What would it be like to study animal tracks without going out on a nature trail to find some? Or geological rock formations without heading to the beach to spend the day playing on large formations of coquina rock? Or snowflakes without pausing from regularly scheduled activities to build a snowman and have a snowball fight (and maybe grab a handful of snow to check out under a microscope)? These types of planned pauses intensify the experiences. They make room for more surprise and a greater level of observation and involvement with what we're studying or learning.

Now, sometimes we study things that we don't get to experience in person until much later, if at all, and that's okay. Sometimes, the pauses are not necessarily to go anywhere special but simply to spend some time processing or enjoying something before moving on. Maybe you read a story and then pause from your routine to watch the movie adaptation. Maybe you learn a new math concept and then pause to play games that reinforce that concept for a week before continuing in your curriculum. Perhaps you create a weekly ritual that intentionally sets aside time to tarry a bit in surprise and wonder, doing more of just about anything that invites it.

One example of this is the Poetry Teatime that so many homeschoolers are familiar with. Here is a beautiful description of it from Brave Writer, which popularized the practice:

> Poetry Teatime offers you and your children a break from the fast-paced demands of homeschooling, parenting, and household running. Everyone sighs a collective "ahhhh" as they settle into their chairs, tea cups or mugs in hand, poetry books scattered across the table. Stopping the rush for a restorative cup of tea (or hot chocolate or cider or coffee or lemonade or juice) creates the perfect space to contemplate rhymes and riddles, limericks and sonnets. When you pair poetry with tea, your children create a connection between

contemplation and rest, while also creating memories of serenity and joy.[6]

Visiting Places in Your Community

We encounter surprises when we venture out into our communities, whether we've planned for them or not. For example, my children and I were invited to attend a day-long living history exhibit not far from where we live. It was put together by a local nonprofit called the Florida Frontiersmen, dedicated to "preserv[ing] the skills, trades, and history of pre-1840 America."[7] It was such a great way to stop and interact with a past we had only read about before. There were many moments of surprise and opportunities to marvel.

We had a similar experience the first time we visited Fort Mose, which was once the first legally sanctioned free Black settlement in the United States. Fort Mose Historic State Park now houses a small museum and a living history exhibit about the people who lived there. After the visit, one of my children commented on how the story of the place is full of surprising facts. Visiting this exhibit allowed us to explore the complexities of the relationships among free Black residents, Spanish settlers, and Yamasee allies—relationships often omitted from traditional history books.

We are usually met by surprises when we visit places like these and stay for a while, and when we come back, there are always new surprises. In the same way that we can reread texts or revisit stories, we can repeatedly return to places that beckon us to hang around and simply be amazed.

Field trips can be closer to home as well. One day, while out on a walk, my children and I passed the main office of a local newspaper. They started asking all kinds of questions about newspapers, so when we got home, I called around and managed to arrange a visit to the paper's printing plant. Communities have so much to offer when you think about the stories, activities, and personal experiences of those who organize, operate, or attend its spaces and places—banks, parks, grocery stores, libraries, universities, hospitals, fire stations, cultural centers, restaurants, markets, malls, schools, places of worship, animal shelters, train stations, post offices, nurseries, and on and on. There are so many places just waiting to surprise you.

Honoring Stories

I can still remember moments from my childhood of being completely lost in the pages of a book. There were books I read that marked me forever. I once asked my children to tell me about the books they've read that strongly impacted them. Most of the books they mentioned were ones that seemed to increase their self-awareness and empathy toward others. In a way, they honored those stories by allowing the words to surprise and affect them. I just love the potential of story to do that. Every time we open a book, it's loaded with possibilities. It's why we read a wide range of authors, topics, genres, settings, perspectives, and protagonists—each new story is an opportunity to connect, envision, dream, learn, and grow.

In her book *A Place to Belong*, homeschooler Amber O'Neal Johnston writes about the importance of reading widely:

> We can't just move through life expecting a diversity of messages to penetrate through osmosis. Our families need to actively seek expansion of thought and communion by looking beyond common conceptions of diversity. And while some fail to recognize or acknowledge the incredible diversity *within* groups of people, insiders are quick to let you know that they're not all the same.[8]

If we only study or make time for what we know or think we know, we are truly missing out on rich learning experiences. If we invite the stories of others into our homes, we automatically make room to be surprised. Poet and children's fiction writer Kwame Alexander said in a 2016 interview, "I'm going to write windows, I'm going to write mirrors, I'm going to write books that are going to elevate and empower young people, to help them become more human."[9] Authors unfold surprise after surprise, and they take us on a journey that we want to join.

The same is true for stories we encounter in real life outside of literature. My children and I completed a project that helped us to see the intersection of familiar people's stories and historical timelines. I wrote about my intent in a Wild + Free article:

> I . . . wanted a concrete way to represent some simple ideas—that people are connected to people, that our stories don't exist in a vacuum, that our wanting to know intersects with someone's knowing, and that creates a connection and understanding that matters. Scholars have said that studying history and the diversity of human experience provides a context from which to understand ourselves and others. So, I began with the voices and experiences of those around us and came up with this weaving project.[10]

We collected fabric scraps from family members and friends that reminded them of past personal events or held some sort of significance for a story they wanted to share with us. They sent us their scraps and the written or oral stories that accompanied them, which they related to us through letters, audio and video recordings, or conversations. My children and I then cut the fabric scraps into strips and wove them onto a large loom. We wove while reading, watching, or listening to the stories together. All the while, we talked, laughed, and sometimes cried.

Most importantly, we did something that caused us to pay better attention to the people in our lives. Stories live everywhere. They are in and around us and on the pages of things we read. If we remain willing to be surprised, we can gradually increase our desire to hear old stories, new stories, difficult stories, triumphant stories, everyday stories, and everything in between.

Conversations

Conversations can lead us to wonder and surprise. They are a powerful tool for tuning into others and actively offering your own ideas, which often leads to something new and unexpected, possibly pleasant or possibly uncomfortable (the makings of a potential growth or learning opportunity).

Scholar, critic, and social activist bell hooks believed that knowledge can be built corporately within a community of thinkers and ideas. She wrote in her book *Teaching Critical Thinking* about the role of conversation in the classroom, saying that "the future of learning lies with the cultivation of conversations, of dialogue"[11] and that "conversation is always about giving. Genuine conversation is about the sharing of power and knowledge; it is fundamentally a cooperative enterprise."[12]

I can't be the only one who has asked my child a question, pretending to be authentically conversing but actually expecting a particular answer. Is anyone else guilty? What if the next time you approached a new text or concept with your child, you had a genuine conversation about it and shared perspectives in a way that was absent of the assumption that you were automatically right? I think a lot would probably be revealed about how the child makes sense of the subject and has come to know what they know.

Partnering with our children through conversation levels the playing field, so to speak, and goes back to the ideal environment for responding to surprise that I discussed at the opening of this section: safety and lack of judgment. We can add our adult insight in a way that doesn't discount the child's. We can allow relationship and connection to be the driving force that stimulates each other's understanding of ideas. An advantage to being at home is that we can push the pause button on these conversations at any time and continue them indefinitely.

Your community of thinkers can even include the works and ideas of others. For example, the writing, music, and art we enjoy are expressions of someone else's thinking and can be added to the rich conversations we have with our children. The exchange of thoughts and feelings happens when, in hooks's words, "we engage in internal critical reflection, internal conversations that give fresh expression to common thought."[13] We can interact with their ideas and make connections that nurture our own thoughts.

Flexibility

Many homeschoolers already operate within some type of flexible arrangement. They decide what their workdays will include and how long they will last. They take time off when they want to. They decide how much time they'll spend on activities. They choose the methods that work best for their children. These arrangements were all created for reasons like making the family functional, keeping everyone happy, and making sure motivation stays high. When families point to the freedom that homeschooling allows, flexibility is usually part of the equation. For us as parents, flexibility allows us to maintain autonomy in how we approach education. Tuning into it will always prompt us to create the balance that works for us and our families.

But there are some other aspects of flexibility worth considering too. When I think about having the greatest level of openness for learning, one of the first things that comes to mind is flexible thinking. So, in this section, I'll discuss flexibility in two different senses, one having to do with our children's cognitive behaviors and the other with our thinking about education. I'll begin with the former.

Sparking Curiosity

The Child Mind Institute describes flexible thinking as "the ability to think about things in a new or different way. It helps us deal with uncertainty, solve problems, adjust to changes, and incorporate new information into our plans and ideas."[14] Flexibility in one's thinking happens when one is open to applying new ideas and is intellectually curious. When we slow down, we make time for curiosity, lingering over a given topic and wondering what something is, what it can do, what it can become, why or how it happened, or how long it will last. Often a simple question breeds more questions.

Once my children unexpectedly found a snakeskin while running around on a playground. They immediately became curious about it, and as I watched them, I realized some things about the posture of curiosity that they had assumed:

- First, they had an emotional response. What they found caused excitement. When we live in a curious state, we allow ourselves to react to what it is we're noticing. We tune into that emotional response and experience things with all our senses.

- Second, they made connections to other related experiences and information they had about the subject. They talked about other snakes they knew of and what they knew about how the process of shedding happens. Curiosity helps us to make connections that draw us toward better understanding.

- Third, they argued. Their arguments over the validity of each other's information caused them to observe more closely. Curiosity forces us to get to know things better, even when what we're seeing causes confusion or disagreement.

- Fourth, the longer my children observed, the more curious they became. They realized there was more that they wanted to know. Curiosity breeds more curiosity. When we live in that place, it becomes our modus operandi.

• Lastly, they walked away from the experience with enthusiasm about their discovery and more questions than answers. Curiosity causes a fascination and enthusiasm that transcends the need to have finite answers.

So how exactly can we prepare an environment for ourselves and for our children that encompasses all that curiosity involves? How can we make our homes places that invite children to question, wonder, and explore? How do we hold space for ideas to flourish?

There is not one generic answer, but I think one way we can do it is by anticipating and celebrating what educator Eleanor Duckworth calls "the virtues of not knowing." In her essay collection *The Having of Wonderful Ideas*, Duckworth describes a scene in which a class was learning about pendulums by watching recordings of a pendulum that "dropped sand as it moved, thus leaving a record of its travels."[15] The students considered the question, "When a pendulum is swinging back and forth, does it slow down at each end of its swing, or does it maintain the same speed and simply change direction?"[16]

Ten-year-old Alec, who was generally thoughtful, creative, and diligent, thought that the pendulum didn't slow down, and at first, other students agreed, because they trusted his instincts. But little by little, students challenged his idea by raising questions about the sand: Why wasn't the sand the same in every location? Why was there more piled up at the ends? How come it wasn't piled up in the middle? One child asserted that it probably passed quickly over the middle and then slowed down at both ends because it couldn't actually stop without slowing down.[17] The other children were right in the end, but they would never have arrived at their ideas without taking the risk of challenging someone else's idea. Duckworth concludes that "the virtues involved in not knowing are the ones that really count in the long run. What you do about what you don't know is, in the final analysis, what determines what you will ultimately know."[18]

Another way we invite this kind of activity is by getting comfortable with questions even more than with answers. This is very different from the standard approach of telling children exactly what they should know or do. The thing is, ambiguity can be uncomfortable, and not rushing to answer our children's questions or standing witness as they draw faulty conclusions is often difficult to do. Not everyone even believes learning how to pursue knowledge can be more important than producing the "right answer." I don't think we get more comfortable with ambiguity by avoiding it. Instead, I think we need more of it to experiment with what it can become, discomfort and all.

Embrace the Question

I've gotten into the habit of jotting down the questions my children ask, keeping a running list in a note on my phone. We refer to it often, sometimes picking one question to spend time exploring. As we do, either interest wanes or full-fledged investigations ensue. Exploring their questions is fabulous practice for chasing ideas that are original to them.

Do you want to know how to kill that spark of wonder almost immediately? Choose something from the list and "make them" research it, insisting it's "their idea." We might be tempted to tell our children exactly how to go about finding out answers. We might even be convinced that we should find out all the information ourselves in the name of "planning." Do you know what's worked out much better?

- Choosing something from the list and investigating together. ("Together" implies a balance of participation when it comes to input, research, and activities.)

- Picking something from their list that's truly interesting to me so that I can set out on a solo journey of finding out, inviting them to join me if they wish.

- Simply keeping the list handy to refer to when and if they ask.

- Talking about and adding to the list often to demonstrate how cool I think their questions are and how smart they are for asking.

- Examining the list together to help them notice abiding interests from the connected themes and frequency of the questions.

- Discussing the list and evaluating it for questions no longer worth exploring, better served by a simple internet search, or already answered after time has passed (their evaluations, not mine).

These questions have led us to studies about things like bridges, architectural design, local wildflowers, and the human body. My sons once wrote a letter to a brain scientist, listing their most pressing questions, which I thought was resourceful of them. I helped them find an address, and they greatly anticipated a response, checking the mailbox daily for the next month. Unfortunately, they never heard back, but I was delighted that their tenacity in finding answers to their questions did not waver.

When I was a classroom teacher, my students and I engaged in many studies that were driven by inquiry. We would usually begin by choosing a broad topic and having a lot of conversations to find out what the students knew already and what they wanted to know. There was one year that the entire school, from pre-K all the way to sixth grade, was studying ancient Egypt. The vastness of the study subject made it possible for a wide range of interests and questions to emerge. Before long, students were researching hieroglyphic writing, ancient number systems, pharaohs and kings, economy, and agriculture. They were constructing pyramids, making paper, sculpting pottery, creating jewelry, and building their own senet gameboards. Together, we were reading various texts and observing artifacts. The study seemed to take on a life of its own, and there were many opportunities for children to share what they were learning. It was an exciting atmosphere to be a part of that was fueled by curiosity.

It was the type of environment that could easily be replicated at home or among a group of friends. If the thought of that sounds overwhelming, note that in that school, we only attempted a school-wide study of this magnitude about once a year. You certainly don't have to study everything this way, but you could plan to dive deeply into a particularly engaging topic in an extensive way once in a while. Think "unit study" but a lot more open-ended, driven mostly by interests, questions, and curiosity. Don't be afraid to linger with questions and allow the uncertainty to be the groundwork for new ideas to flow.

Classical education tradition trains students in practicing the "Five Common Topics of Dialectic," which are meant to help students ask questions in such a way that new subjects can be thoroughly explored. The topics are as follows:

- **Definition:** questions that help discover and define what something means or entails

- **Comparison:** questions that seek out similarities, differences, and the significance of each

- **Relationship:** questions that try to understand how one thing is related to another, causes and effect, and where inconsistencies lie

- **Circumstance:** questions that consider what is and isn't possible or probable and what connections there are to other ideas or events

- **Testimony:** questions that seek to find credible sources[19]

These dialectic topics are designed to help students wrestle with ideas and become more accustomed to the tension that exists inside of not knowing.

Similarly, Socratic questioning has been a longtime practice in schools and universities. The modern approach to this method uses dialogue through thoughtful questioning to encourage the examination of ideas with logic and reasoning. Dr. Richard Paul, a major advocate for critical thinking across every grade level, offered a taxonomy of Socratic questions to help guide teachers, professionals, and students: "questions of clarification, questions that probe assumptions, questions that probe reasons and evidence, questions about viewpoints or perspectives, questions that probe implications and consequences, and questions about the question."[20]

Here is an example of the types of questions[21] that go with each category:

CLARIFICATION:

What do you mean by _____?
What is the main issue?
Can you explain _____?

ASSUMPTIONS:

Is that always true?
Why would someone assume _____?
Could we assume instead?

REASONS AND EVIDENCE:

How does that apply?

How do you know?

Is there a reason to question this evidence?

VIEWPOINTS OR PERSPECTIVES:

What's the alternative?

How would someone respond who believed _____?

Why have you chosen this perspective?

IMPLICATIONS AND CONSEQUENCES:

Are you implying _____?

What effect does that have?

If we say _____, then how about _____?

QUESTIONS ABOUT THE QUESTION:

Why is this question important?

Are there any assumptions within this question?

Are there parts of the question that are unclear?

Inquiry and asking deeper questions are skills that can be practiced together with your children and improved over time. Just be wary of making a chore of questioning everything instead of approaching material in a way that would make one more curious. Model your own way of asking questions, and couch the questions you ask your children inside of a genuine conversation. Ask your questions and let your children ask theirs while taking a walk together with the dog, sipping iced tea, or on a trip to the grocery store. Avoid asking rapid-fire questions and calling it conversation.

There's no special recipe to make someone more curious than they already innately are. All we can do is create circumstances that will hopefully prompt a curious reaction. When people conduct science experiments with children, they do this quite naturally. Think of a science teacher who has asked a group of children to place an egg in a jar of vinegar. The next day they check the egg only to discover that the shell can easily be wiped away (if it's not gone already), leaving the membrane exposed.

Everyone in the room probably begins to ask questions and hypothesize about the answers. What happened to the shell? What is the eggshell made of? Why does the egg look larger? How is the membrane that strong? Could this happen in water too? Some might even begin to say things they noticed along the way. There were bubbles in the jar when the egg was in it. The egg now feels rubbery. The science teacher has successfully gotten those children to notice a phenomenon that they became curious about. The more questions they have, the more they realize they don't have all the answers, and the more curious they become.

This doesn't work only with science. The first time I read with my daughter two different accounts of the story of Pocahontas, one from the perspective of people of the Powhatan Nation and another from a children's book that told Disney's version, she noticed the discrepancies. In effect, I directed her attention to something ambiguous, and her curiosity was piqued.

Children don't always know what to do with their curiosity or how best to satisfy their desire to know or understand. This is where we come in to lend the support that they need. We may need to be the listening ear as they talk through their ponderings. Maybe we choose to offer our adult perspective. Perhaps we point them toward more information. We might keep the curiosity going by together observing details or evidence that are just as puzzling.

Even questions that can be answered definitively have some degree of nuance that is worth investigating further. We need time to sit with ideas and rework them if necessary. Perspectives can be broadened and complexity honored when we're not rushing to make the learning in our homes picture-perfect.

Cultivating Creativity and Imagination

Another aspect of flexible thinking is creativity. One way to think of creativity is as the expression of curiosity; curiosity can be voiced or revealed by creativity or creative pursuits. As you allow yourself space for exploration and imagination, you can both express existing curiosity and reveal new curiosity. People can be curious about a whole lot of things, but they don't necessarily chase it with creativity. For that, courage is required.

Cultivating creativity as an expression of curiosity means becoming more and more comfortable with the idea of imagination. So many of us are okay with it for young children, but somehow, we've bought into the idea that as they get older, these fanciful forays of the mind need to be exchanged for more serious intellectual endeavors. Laura Grace Weldon, the author of *Free Range Learning*, writes that "imagination springs from nowhere and brings something new to the world—games, art, inventions, stories, solutions. Childhood is particularly identified with this state, perhaps because creativity in adults is considered to be a trait possessed only by the artistic few."[22] But we all have creative potential. It's an ability that can be developed through experimentation.

Imagination is the process of forming new ideas, images, and even concepts that the senses don't necessarily have a reference for. It allows the mind to form a vision of something that may not already exist. It is the precursor to every innovative idea or invention. Through imagination, we can experience other viewpoints and become fascinated by all we have yet to understand. It inches us closer to caring for the world around us.

I like the way that Keith Sawyer, author of *Explaining Creativity*, describes creativity in improvisational theater:

In improv, actors intentionally speak lines of dialogue that are ambiguous, utterances that can be interpreted in multiple ways. Actors do this on purpose—not because they're lazy thinkers, or they're just trying to fill up time. Improvising these ambiguous actions takes a lot of creativity. It's not easy to say something that opens up possibilities for the scene, and doesn't close down possible futures, but something that also provides enough specifics to drive a scene forward, to give other actors something to work with.[23]

If we think about education as a sort of improv experiment, our job as fellow actors is saying lines that invite possibilities. We're inviting our children to take risks and explore in a way that pushes their creativity. Here are a few ideas for doing that.

OBSERVING ART AND GROUP ART

Observing art can help boost your creativity. Taking time to look at it in new ways can broaden your perspective on the world. Choose a piece of visual art to observe. It can be the piece itself or a photo of it. Begin analyzing it by asking how the artist might have made it, what choices the artist made in creating it, and what features help answer these questions (like materials, concepts, shapes, subject matter, perspective, light, movement, scale, etc.). Also consider what makes the work interesting, unique, or different. Tailor the depth of your discussion to the age of your participants.

Alternatively, create a group art piece. Sculptures (made of clay, paper, recycled materials, or the like) work well for this, as do drawings, paintings, or collages. Each person should take turns adding their own part. Ironically, sometimes the less time is allotted to do a collaborative project like this, the more flexible your thinking has to be. It's fun to experiment with time and to process together afterward with the people involved, discussing exactly how they went about accomplishing the finished work and what types of compromises, accommodations, cooperation, and openness were required.

APPLY NEW KNOWLEDGE TO SOMETHING ELSE

There are many ways that applying new knowledge can happen. It can be as simple as learning how to add money and then using grocery receipts to figure out how much was spent in a week; practicing literary analysis with a picture book and then later repeating that same practice with a longer, more challenging text; applying the principles of physics learned from a book to exploration with spinning tops; or studying how government works in America and how it's similar or different to how things work in other countries. When we have an opportunity to compare different scenarios, it helps us to see information that transfers from one context to another.

Applying new knowledge can also occur when we teach a newly gained skill or explain something we've learned to someone else, perhaps a younger sibling. Transferring what we know to a different format, like documenting an idea or concept through a photography journal, is another creative way of representing our understanding of something. Similarly, creating a new version of something like a 3D model to show how it works (or an entirely new design to show how it could work better) is an example of using the imagination to apply knowledge.

BRAINSTORMING POSSIBLE SOLUTIONS

Instead of focusing on the correct answer, present problems and ask your children to propose different ways of solving them. While they're brainstorming, write down all their ideas without filtering out the ones you think won't work. You can rehearse this without belaboring the practice. Every now and then, simply make the methods used to solve the problems the most important thing. Highlight the process more than the answer.

For each option, together, talk through the steps and why you're making them, especially if they include a line of thinking that isn't explicit. Model this a great deal if your children have trouble contributing to this kind of conversation. Ask questions to help move their thinking along if they get stuck. At these moments, cultivate an atmosphere in which it's okay to be wrong. Once you've done this, it may become obvious that some methods work better than others.

It isn't necessary to come up with a solution. You're zeroing in on how they got there. For children who are bothered by not arriving at a definitive answer, you can start this whole process by revealing the answer and still focus on different ways of arriving at the solution. This activity lends itself well to subjects that already integrate problem-solving.

Curriculum

Flexible thinking helps us to solve problems and to think creatively. It involves features that bring the mind to life and help learning come alive. Vito Perrone, an innovator in teaching and learning, wrote that "such a perspective demands a curriculum that truly challenges young people, that is laden with questions and multiple possibilities for entry and for active learning. It suggests, as well, time to observe, sit, think, and rework ideas."[24] If the curriculum you're using isn't explicit in the ways it encourages flexible thinking, then you'll have to infuse it on your own.

Ideally, we control the educational process, using a curriculum as a tool to support us. Yet there are people who feel their curriculum puts them in somewhat of a gilded cage. They're attracted by the curriculum's promise of ease and exhaustive coverage, only to find themselves trapped by its irrational and overwhelming demands. It ceases to be a resourceful aid and instead becomes a source of anxiety. The curriculum begins to call the shots, and the users reluctantly oblige. It's time to settle the fact that it does not have the power we pretend it does.

Have you ever used a curriculum and felt compelled to do everything in it exactly the way it was written? You knew good and well that doing it *all* was unrealistic and just way too much material, but you attempted it anyway. In some cases, the surplus is meant to provide you with multiple entry points. The many examples and activities might exist to appeal to different children's unique ways of thinking and make it easier for you to choose. Once there's a way in, you can then customize your options and create space for your children to do work that interests, challenges, or delights them. Don't let curriculum overwhelm you. Learning can't always be packaged neatly, even when using one.

I have some confessions to make that I hope won't rattle you too much (especially if you have a "Type A" personality). In my family, we typically don't pay attention to the levels and grades that are marked on our math curriculum. We start from a place that makes sense, and we work through it at a pace that feels natural. When my son and I agreed that he was ready for a bit more challenge in his math work, we were at the end of a particular level book. For some reason, even though I thought we owned it, I couldn't find the book for the next level, so we just jumped right in on the level that came after that. When we encountered things he didn't know, we just parked there for a bit and did things to shore up his understanding. As the adage goes: *Teach the child, not the curriculum.*

When my daughter read through a scope and sequence presentation of all the math concepts typically encountered before high school, she decided that the amount she still had left to cover before starting ninth grade was way more than what she expected. She asked me to help her make a daily plan that would allow her to work on all the topics in the space of about a year and a half. She basically wanted to double the amount of math that we normally did. (This was no small feat, as she has dyscalculia.) I looked through all the math lessons and picked out the most essential. We skipped some topics that I knew we could easily revisit later. We opted for doing ten of the twenty problems on the worksheet to keep things moving at an appropriate pace.

Along the way, we adjusted her timeline as necessary. *Teach the child, not the curriculum.*

When we grew tired of the repetition toward the end of another child's math curriculum book, I stopped using it three-quarters of the way through. I gave him the end-of-the-year test to see what areas were strong and where he needed more development. We tossed the curriculum (in a metaphorical sense) and just played games and did math projects together for a couple of weeks in the hopes of targeting some of those areas. Then we just moved to the next level. *Teach the child, not the curriculum.*

This also happens outside of math. I once stretched a history curriculum meant to last one school year over three years. We went through it, making connections to other bodies of knowledge and other books, deepening our experience every step of the way. We repeated books and revisited texts when it was necessary to help build understanding. We moved slowly, seeking out artifacts and primary sources, open to learning about the world and hearing the stories of the people in it. We did work we were proud of. The amount of material we "covered" in one year might have been a lot less than what was typical, but that was of no consequence in comparison with what we gained in the process.

So what makes a curriculum "work"? Well, the truth is, there is no perfect curriculum. There are many families that homeschool without one. But if you do use one and refuse to deviate from it, you're probably missing out on some important learning opportunities. What if your child unexpectedly latches on to something within the curriculum but you rush them to move on because the curriculum guide says to devote two weeks only? Or what if it's the opposite and both you and your child find yourselves drudging through a topic that fails to spark any excitement at all? In both scenarios, there is a lack of dynamism and flexibility.

I imagine that people don't think they'll encounter many problems when they research and purchase a curriculum that holds a lot of promise, but when springtime rolls around and they start taking inventory of the year, they find it didn't live up to their expectations. I've talked to other parents who feel like they change curriculum with the wind. This can happen in the name of trying to find the "right fit" for the child, but I also think it can be an effort to use the materials as an answer to a plaguing question: How can I simplify my life and make this homeschool thing as easy as possible?

Interestingly, I think that the answer to that question doesn't come through curriculum; it can only be found within ourselves. Many of us are tired, stressed, maybe even burnt out, and looking for ways to engage our children that require the least amount of extra work for us—less preparation, less mental energy. While this is the reality we face, there is no way around investing time where and when it's necessary.

Perhaps the more appropriate question is: What is this curriculum requiring of me, and is it asking me to spend my time in ways that I value? What is it that I want to be doing with my child when we carve out time for history, math, or writing? Is the work even presented in an interesting way? Do I want to struggle, argue, and "get through" with complete disinterest on the child's part, or do I want to spend our time in more meaningful ways? Perhaps that should be our main criteria for any curriculum we use.

Or we could endeavor to use curriculum materials in a way that preserves joy, no matter what we are using. We must maintain control over that curriculum, rather than the other way around. Our approach and mindset about aligning learning with our values should have more influence over our day than what any curriculum can prescribe.

Stop Speeding Up Slow Processes

We have the advantage of being able to incorporate flexible scheduling into our day, but every so often, instead of adopting a relaxed way of approaching daily tasks, we can find ourselves hurrying school along to move on to the fifty other things we need to do. I get it. I mean, who else is going to go to the grocery store, make dinner, or vacuum the floor? However, sometimes in our haste, we forget that there are things that we just can't speed up.

Oliver Burkeman, in his book *Four Thousand Weeks*, notes that reading is one of those things. Explaining how reading is something people often complain about not having time for, he writes:

> It's not so much that we're too busy, or too distractible, but that we're unwilling to accept the truth that reading is the sort of activity that largely operates according to its own schedule. You can't hurry it very much before the experience begins to lose its meaning; it refuses to consent, you might say, to our desire to exert control over how our time unfolds. In other words, and in common with far more aspects of reality than we're comfortable acknowledging, reading something properly just takes the time it takes.[25]

Educator and historian Susan Wise Bauer concurs: "Reading is a lifelong process. There's no hurry, no semester schedule, no end-of-term panic, no final exam. The idea that fast reading is good reading is a twentieth-century weed, springing out of the stony farmland cultivated by the computer manufacturers."[26] It is unsettling to think that the impatience that Burkeman and Bauer describe might be the reason so many people struggle to read with any of the critical analysis necessary for tackling difficult texts full of complex ideas.

Julie Bogart, in her book *Raising Critical Thinkers*, describes an antidote to the shallow perusal of texts: deep reading. Deep reading is "choosing to engage in a sustained way. Reading for depth—giving patient consideration to an idea. . . . Deep reading means no one is expecting you to comment—at least, not right away. The internal dialogue . . . between text and reader can be rich and unedited."[27]

What are some other things we do or ask our children to do that require patience or close, thoughtful attention? What other processes have focus and possibly reflection built in? What are skills we want to help our children improve that are practiced with high levels of concentration? What other kinds of academic activities are akin to deep reading?

How about writing an essay that requires deep thinking and careful composition of thoughts? Or solving a complicated math problem with information and parts that must be examined carefully and systematically? What about preparing for a debate that requires substantial, high-quality research? Or doing a science experiment with many steps and related information you need to reread in order to understand? Completing a history project or map work that demands accuracy and thorough investigation? Learning a new musical piece on the piano by reading sheet music?

When my children and I began a self-paced course in brush drawing (a watercolor and ink technique), we practiced by using a series of exercises meant to develop better brush control. We did our best work when we were quiet, relaxed, and focused on the strokes we were making. In fact, when one child talked too much or interrupted the peace with occasional chatter, another would ask for silence. It was impossible to rush or to give only part of our attention while making the brushstrokes correctly.

A flexible approach to time will help us stop trying to speed up processes that are meant to be experienced slowly. Some things just take the time they take, and patience and resilience are required. One thing we can do as parents is to stop interrupting. When we notice that our children are in a flow, doing something demanding with a great level of focused attention, there is no need to stop them prematurely. This is different from "keeping lessons short" to sustain maximum attention, which is a choice we make to do less in the name of good judgment. The key is allowing our children to work deeply on academic activities without rushing, rather than hurrying them along while at the same time demanding concentration and precision. As with deep reading, we can develop the habit of close attention a little at a time, gradually increasing the time we encourage our children to sustain their focus.

In her book about teaching math to young children, educator and former astronaut Julia Brodsky encourages allowing for "thinking time" to help students think deeply about complex problems for increasingly long periods:

> Students can only give answers when the thinking time is over. Students may enjoy using a big sandglass or a timer. Remind those who rush to answer before the time is over to capture their thoughts (write, doodle, build). This way, you teach the students to focus on the problem, and to take time to consider alternative solutions. They also learn how to deal with impatience.[28]

When we accept that we can't always control the time that things take to engage deeply, we can be ready for opportunities as they come rather than hurrying all schoolwork along. We can choose flexibility instead and the development of perseverance that goes along with deep work. Our children will learn that it is possible to practice persistence even alongside their limitations.

Uncover the Subjects

Contrary to common belief, "covering the subjects" is not our mission. *Uncovering* the subjects is the venture worth taking. To simply "cover" a subject means we feel a responsibility to incorporate it into our course of study. We run the risk of that coverage being cursory if we're only including it out of a sense of duty. "Uncovering" a subject means looking at it closely, turning it upside down and inside out to know it better. It means we're willing to confront fears and strip away misconceptions about a particular field. We go beyond surface-level understanding and try to expose the subject for what it really is. We ask questions like: What are all the kinds of thinking involved in this academic area? It is only X, Y, and Z, or is there more? What do professionals in this field actually do? Is that even close to how we're experiencing it at home?

I love talking to math professionals who have dedicated themselves to sharing play-based, deep-inquiry math endeavors with children. They've taught me about math circles, groups of people who gather together to experience math in fun, collaborative, interactive ways. Meetings can happen anywhere, even online. What strikes me is that many of the adults leading math circles are professors, math Ph.D.s, engineers, and scientists who say that something is seriously lacking in our children's math education. The formal education happening across schools is not always as interesting or engaging as the field itself, and the rote learning of mathematical processes doesn't necessarily show a deep understanding of mathematical concepts. Math is so much more than arithmetic functions. These adults are looking for ways to go back and reteach the math, helping children to have better math experiences. They're essentially modeling ways one can uncover the subject.

Educator Deborah Meier, describing how the classes in her school were set up, writes, "We decided that students needed lots of opportunities to practice science, not just to hear about it; to be writers, not just do writing exercises; to read books, not just practice becoming readers; as well as to do history, make ideas, and care about their world by working in it."[29] These ideas highlight sharp differences in educational approaches. What we think our children need will affect which opportunities we make space for in any learning environment. How many ways can a subject be uncovered? It's probably endless! But we first need to settle into a pace that welcomes the practice.

Think about how things are presented in a textbook versus how they might be explained or spoken about by people who are passionately working in that field, like an artist, geographer, or editor. What kinds of experiences would an artist think are important to have in order to study art? How do they compare to what's in your home-school art manual? Would a geographer only discuss the features of a map and general facts about landforms and water bodies, or might their work also involve posing important questions to help with urban planning or organizing a focus group to collect detailed data? We ask children to edit their writing, but those working in the editing field employ a broad set of skills. How might we help a child take any piece of writing (not necessarily their own) and propose ways of better communicating the ideas? These are skills that can't all be taught in a "unit." They take years to develop as students uncover a subject.

Overlap the Disciplines

Flexibility also extends to the overlapping of disciplines. You don't have to choose between uncovering a single subject and overlapping multiple disciplines. You can do both if you stay flexible and seize the opportunities as they come—maybe not every time, but certainly more often.

I've seen teachers attempt to make their classroom study units more interdisciplinary by simply incorporating activities related to the disciplines they're weaving in. So, for example, they choose to study oceans and then divide their room into learning centers where students can do things like solving word problems about oceans (math), drawing ocean animals (art), reading poems about oceans (literature), spelling ocean-related words (spelling), or writing about ocean activity (writing).

However, when we look at the world and the issues in it, they are not divided into separate disciplines. They are accessible in more ways than zeroing in on one at a time. If an earthquake devastated a region, engineering, medicine, economics, and civics could all be at play at once; while an engineer was working to redesign roads, a doctor could be performing surgery on the survivor of a building collapse, and a humanitarian organization could be raising money for relief workers. It is possible to examine something from the perspective of multiple disciplines.

So rather than trying to make what we're studying fit neatly into subject area–related activities, why not look for overlap that relates more closely to how events play out naturally in the world around us? We can take an issue and ask questions like: How might a scientist think about this issue? What about a historian, an artist, a filmmaker, or an economist? What questions might they ask? What information would they rely on? What would be the end result of their work?

Things Might Not Be Like You Planned

Finally, we need the flexibility to be wrong and to change our minds. Homeschooling is a journey that is impossible to map out perfectly from the start. It's a given that we'll have to adjust along the way. But the times when we're wrong or must modify our steps are never wasted. Flexibility will lend the support that we need to homeschool boldly.

When we first started homeschooling, for example, I decided that the main language I would use to do so would be French. I was already speaking French to my children at home, so I thought it was a natural progression for my first child to learn to read in French, to have a French math book, and for all of our resource books to be in French. The only problem was that acquiring all these French books was not always easy. I had a lot of help from French-speaking family members, made use of every free resource I could find, and made a lot of my own materials, but it was still an expensive endeavor. In the end, we had to alter our approach. I still prioritized being bilingual, but we needed flexibility to really work out the details of how that would look for our family. We've made countless other decisions like this when we realized that we were wrong and needed to change course.

Things might not always be like you planned, but you should also make plans for the things you like. If one of my children woke up and asked me if we could spend all day reading in a variety of ways, I would be hard-pressed to say no. If they asked me if they could get comfy on the couch and read a book, I would think that sounded pretty amazing. If they asked to listen to our audiobook while driving to the grocery store, I'd say, "Let's do it!" If they wanted to snuggle with me and read picture books, I'd be the first to go grab a stack. If they wanted to listen to me read a couple of pages of our history reading while they were eating lunch, I'd have no complaints.

In my mind, spending a day like this equates to a great day of homeschooling because I myself love reading. But truly, you can have the same sentiment and replace it with anything you love. Take math, for example. You might love math games at breakfast, mini math challenges while baking muffins, verbal math quizzes while driving, a morning of math projects—you get the idea. The point is that who you are and what you love are inevitably going to be a part of what you're creating at home. Some days, you might be leaning into those things more because they feel familiar or because they come easily. Don't be so inflexible about only offering what your child needs that you forget about yourself. You are part of the home experience too.

Spontaneity

This brings us to the final element of learning at a different tempo: spontaneity. I think for many, when they hear the word "spontaneous," the first thing that comes to mind is something unplanned, minimally planned, or without an obvious plan. People labeled spontaneous are thought to be full of life, willing to go with the flow and take risks. Some of us are by nature very spontaneous, while others of us would say that we're not very spontaneous at all. If you're someone who relishes the organization of a well-planned day, you may scoff at the very idea of spontaneity. But, interestingly, I think that spontaneity involves a little bit from both sides of this personality spectrum.

How so? In his book *The Fun Habit*, behavioral scientist Michael

Rucker discusses how, as wonderful as spontaneity is, it's still something that we need to create space for: "We often mistakenly think that 'magical moments' shouldn't require planning. While it's true that magical moments are nearly impossible to contrive, you do have to commit to making space for them in your life. To do so effectively takes planning and discipline."[30]

But if spontaneity is, to some extent, something we can plan for, is it really spontaneity? Yes, because spontaneity is not defined only by a lack of planning; another way to define it is "proceeding from natural feeling or native tendency."[31] What would a "natural" response be, in an educational environment, if you were uninhibited by worry, pressure, or other constraints? I personally would be more engaged and "in the moment." I would be much more reflective on my experiences. I would be more intentional about my work and do things either slowly or quickly, as the work warranted or as I saw fit. In a learning context, spontaneity would be the thing that could possibly help me experience what I am engaged in with more vibrancy and intensity.

Experience a "Long Breath" Moment

One day, at the close of a particularly good story that I was reading together with some of my children, we all sat in silence thinking. After a long moment, one son started clapping intensely. Then he said, "Hey, did you ever notice how at the end of really good books and movies, there's this long breath that you need to take? You have to get quiet and take it all in." I knew exactly what he meant. It's a very natural response to take a moment and contemplate something that affected you deeply. It's why people sit quietly just staring at the credits of particular movies, or why we exhale slowly when the curtain goes down after a moving scene in a play.

I'll never forget when, during my stint as a substitute high school teacher, I sat among a group of students reading a story aloud to them. The bell rang, and it was time for the next period to start. A voice kept urging me, "Miss, just finish. Keep reading!" There were only a few more pages to go. By the end of the chapter, we were all in tears and no one wanted to move. We had all shared something special, and now we were united through the story. It was as if we had become bonded through our conversations over the last few weeks as the plot unfolded, and we had all emerged just as changed as our book's heroes.

My spontaneous decision to keep my class a little longer that day had consequences that directly affected my colleagues. I'm sure they were not thrilled that the students showed up late for their next periods. However, experiencing a "long breath" moment at home has been easier. We can read (or do just about anything) together and make space for our natural desire to respond and process. We do this often by talking. Sometimes we laugh or argue. Other times, we draw or journal. We allow ourselves time to contemplate and react.

Learn to Draw . . . and Use It for Creative Problem-Solving

Although this may sound odd, learning to draw has helped me to have better natural and creative responses to problems that I encounter. Most of my insight into this has been influenced by Betty Edwards and her book *Drawing on the Right Side of the Brain*, one that I read for the first time over two decades ago. Her work helps you not only to become a better artist but also to use the perceptual skills you practice in drawing in other areas too. She writes:

> This is my major premise: having learned to *know* perceptual skills through actually using them in drawing will enhance your success in transferring your visual skills to thinking and problem solving. *You will see things differently.* For example, once you have actually *seen and drawn* negative spaces, shared edges, angles and proportions, or lights and shadows, the mental concepts become real, and one of the best ways to use the skills is to actually visualize—*see in*

your mind's eye—the edges of a problem, the spaces, relationships, lights and shadows, and the *gestalt* [perception of the whole].[32]

Visual skills can and do transfer to other areas of thinking, even for those who don't consider themselves artistic or skilled at drawing. It's nice to be able to use these skills as a tool when thinking through something. They enrich the range of natural or spontaneous responses we have to all sorts of learning encounters.

Additionally, using drawing skills in an impromptu way can help us assess new information. One of the exercises that Edwards instructs readers to do in her book is to make an upside-down drawing to see lines and the relationship between lines for what they are, rather than what our brains assign them to be simply because they look familiar. We use this exercise every now and then, drawing photographs, art images, and other visual media upside down before we discuss or analyze them. Sometimes we even photograph things we're observing and then we use the photo to make an upside-down drawing.

Slow Down Time with Novelty

Some of my best memories of summertime from when I was a child were lounging around on Caribbean beaches with my cousins, feasting at backyard barbecues with family and friends, and catching fireflies until the streetlights came on. Summers seemed to last forever, and they were full of delightful, endless activity. Michael Easter, in *The Comfort Crisis*, writes about this phenomenon of how children experience time:

New situations kill the mental clutter. In newness we're forced into presence and focus. This is because we can't anticipate what to expect and how to respond, breaking the trance that leads to life in fast forward. Newness can even slow down our sense of time. This explains why time seemed slower when we were kids. Everything was new then and we were constantly learning.[33]

What if we created space for doing new and unexpected things so that we could experience time more slowly? Who wouldn't want to enjoy more time with their children and savor those homeschool moments the same way we did our childhood summers? Spontaneity can be a way to capture the comfort, security, and peace of time moving slowly. It adds just enough novelty to negate the fast feelings that routines can create (the feeling that time is speeding up and there is, therefore, less of it).

When time is scarce, or when there's little time for deviation from your plans, spontaneity can seem impossible. But there are many ways you can weave this element into your school day, and I wanted to give you two examples that we have enjoyed. They might not be new or novel for you, so you might try some different ideas. Much like with the element of surprise, new does not always have to mean unfamiliar. Even doing something familiar in a new way can capture the attention of our children. Similarly, doing something routine or ordinary with increased intensity can be life-giving in new ways. Spontaneity can create memorable moments that exceed our expectations.

- **Create interactive stories, games, and animations:**
  Without much planning, we've used websites like Scratch to create interactive stories, games, and animations together. This particular website includes guides for educators to help them become familiar with what it has to offer. Similarly, sites like Code.org or Tynker offer a platform for learning to code, where many of the resources are free. Sites like Tinkercad teach 3D design and coding. The thing that makes these exploration times special is that I am there exploring along with my children. We're applying academic skills to an area they see as fun and somewhat unexpected.

Because my own level of comfort with these tools isn't as high as with some others, when we do things like this together, it truly is in partnership and collaboration. As a result, my children feel like it is an authentic opportunity to take risks alongside me.

- **Math fun:** After reading Barbara Oakley's *A Mind for Numbers* and her insights into boosting your memory, I started using some of her tips (like creating visual metaphors, spacing out repetitive attempts, making meaningful groups, creating stories, and using muscle memory with movement and exercise)[34] to spontaneously present ways of reinforcing concepts we are working on. We do so playfully and enjoy observing what tips work for one person and what doesn't work for another. In some ways, we're testing out whether the memory tricks will work over time, and the mild skepticism my children have is what keeps things fun. They have happily discovered that so far, many of the tricks do work for them!

The Gift of Time

The time that we have at home with our children is precious. If we're educating them at home, we have unique decisions to make about how we spend our time that extend beyond day-to-day parenting. When we choose to slow down, we reclaim the freedom for our children to learn at the tempo that feels right. Freedom is for us too. When we learn without the limitations that a narrow view of time presents, we instantly create an atmosphere that feels expansive and brimming with possibility. Slow truly is a paradox of balance. It points to the internal peace and stability that comes from deep and meaningful learning but is never one thing (one educational approach, one curriculum, one philosophy of learning) to the exclusion of all else. It is the right thing at the right time for the best result.

I will end this chapter with words from Sharon Draper, an American children's writer and educator who, in an inspirational book for teachers, imagined giving time as a gift in the same way you might give money, on the condition that it be spent every day.

> Each day you have the opportunity to spend that gift of time. And you can buy anything you want with it. What will you buy? . . . It must be spent wisely, carefully, and thoughtfully. For once it is gone it can never be retrieved. What have you done with the hours, the moments, the seconds you have been given thus far? And what will you do with those to come? For the gift I offered you is not hypothetical—it's very real. It is as real as the heart that beats within you. My gift to you is time. Use it wisely. Use it well.[35]

CHAPTER 8

Tools for Measuring Growth

How to Track Progress over Time

Daily practice can feel like drudgery in a results-driven world.
How do we stay the course when the road is long and progress is slow?

—RUTH CHOU SIMONS, *BEHOLDING AND BECOMING*

I have this wonderful memory of about one hundred children singing loudly, their exuberant voices echoing throughout a school auditorium. It was early on a weekday morning. They were belting out the lyrics to "Garden Song," an American folk song written in 1975 by David Mallett: "Inch by inch, row by row, Gonna make this garden grow."[1]

This song always reminds me of how processes require patience. Beautiful gardens aren't built overnight, but what they yield makes the wait worth it. This chapter is about seeing our children's cumulative growth over time and discerning the inches that grow in their educational garden. Why *over time*? Because if we're slowing things down without allowing more time to notice how a child is developing, then I suspect we'll miss a lot of important details.

So how can we capture those details from a point in the middle of the process? How can we document a child's ongoing work and get better at the kind of noticing that honors their freedom to develop at their own pace? How can we reflect on what we notice in ways that seek to know our children better as learners and thinkers? I hope to share with you some tools that might be more appropriate for a slow schooling context. Before we get to those tools, however, I want to discuss how we conventionally conceive of progress and the ways in which we might rethink our assumptions.

Rethinking Time

With more time come more opportunities to deepen one's understanding, even if the progress is slow. Laurent Schwartz, a French mathematician, wrote of his time in school: "I was always deeply uncertain about my own intellectual capacity . . . I was, and still am, rather slow. I need time to seize things because I always need to understand them fully."[2] After years of feeling this way, he finally came to realize that "rapidity doesn't have a precise relation to intelligence. What is important is to deeply understand things and their relations to each other. This is where intelligence lies. The fact of being quick or slow isn't really relevant. Naturally, it's helpful to be quick, like it is to have a good memory. But it's neither necessary or sufficient for intellectual success."[3]

The description of his school experience showed something important. Time is needed not only for the learner to think and process, but also for educators (including parents) to understand the learner's development. Sometimes the process is not quick, and that has nothing to do with a child's intellectual capacity.

Howard Gruber was an educator and psychologist who in 1981 explored the idea that time necessary for thinking was more complex than what most people imagined. He thought that if teachers really gave students a chance to think in a variety of ways, it would necessitate a change in the classroom's pace (slowing it down) and in the teacher's goals (making it about more than cruising through curriculum).

He broke what he saw as the time necessary for learning into five parts. First was the time it took to initially respond to something. Second was the time to form and strengthen a response, with the opportunity to repeat something—not necessarily more quickly, but in a reconstructed way that accounted for prior experiences. Third was the time it took to share responses, to hear responses different from or similar to yours, and to observe where you stood within the diverse range. Fourth was the time for reflection, because every response or answer you give offers the possibility of a new level of investigation. Last was the time involved with the growth of the intellect over longer stretches or intervals.[4]

We can either be the people who seek to extinguish this sort of time or the people who support it by looking at our children's development with a long-range perspective. It would also be important to remember that a learner grows not just in terms of facts they know, tests they ace, concepts they understand, or skills they're using comfortably. Growth encompasses so many more parts of development that sometimes get swept under the rug of academic proficiency (like the ability to persevere, show empathy, be self-aware, be reliable, be confident, demonstrate courage, develop a sense of wonder, or organize work).

We get to see development emerge bit by bit across a broad set of abilities. As with an assortment of seeds scattered in a garden, it's the kind of variety produced by hardiness and fragility existing in proximity. The conditions around learning can create resiliency within the learners.

Rethinking Success

In chapter 7, when I discussed the importance of surprise to learning, I brought up the topic of resiliency. Resiliency takes time to build, and we can often see it developing right alongside other growth markers throughout a child's development. I mentioned psychologists Luna and Renninger's research on how one of the ways we build resilience is by setting attainable goals and helping our children to experience success before asking them to do something much more difficult. While many traditional forms of assessment are only concerned with students getting the right answers (exposing their failure to do so quickly or consistently enough), taking the long view of children's growth offers the chance to see them develop authentic ways of acquiring skills in meaningful contexts in which they encounter both failure and success. Failure and success are not the penalty and prize for children's evaluated performance but rather the data they need to recover, adapt, and move on.

To take things a step further, there has been much educational and psychological research that shows that we associate success with prior incidents of success. There should be enough flexibility in what we're doing with children so that they regularly experience success. We can help our children to experience it by working with them to develop their personal long-term goals for things they care about and that matter to them. We can encourage them in the things they love doing. We can guide them in responsive, helpful ways. We can genuinely lend them our support. Without abdicating leadership, we can partner with them like an ally and a friend. Over time, this will support the process of preparing for challenges that they encounter naturally or that we present in stages.

When we look at how children develop across spans of time, we become less obsessed with measuring them against a timetable and more committed to responsibly occupying the time we have with them. In the early 2000s, a group of educators at an elementary school in Vermont did just that, conducting a series of studies of a child they called Jenny over a period of years. They sought to track a child's development over time while also ensuring that she had many opportunities to accomplish goals in personalized ways. What was remarkable about these studies was that they had a "cumulative yield for Jenny and her family. Each study generated cogent suggestions for supporting Jenny's strengths. Each contributed to a vocabulary apt and specific to Jenny. Each broke the school mold of categorization of individual children according to a generalized standard."[5]

When we take time to think more deeply about our children than what quick assessments allow, we learn things about our children that simply can't be gauged in isolation. We can embed opportunities to carry those continuities across different disciplines and experiences and throughout their learning. Just like in Jenny's case, we can begin to maximize what the process of learning looks like all together.

Rethinking Scope and Sequence

Schools, school districts, educational departments, and curriculum makers have traditionally created what is known as a "scope and sequence" for all the material they plan to cover. They devise what they believe is a reasonable order for planning and presenting curricular content.

When we think about school subjects or academic areas of learning, we often think of them in these terms—a sequential order of study that can only move along in one direction. You could never, for example, explore verb tenses and how they convey time *before* practicing proper punctuation and capitalization—right? Well, I think that just maybe you could. By seeing subjects across a continuum, we can familiarize ourselves with the scope of different academic fields with an understanding that not all subjects need to be learned in a linear way and that there are many different levels of understanding, even when it comes to one single concept or skill.

Take, for example, math. According to mathematician Keith Devlin, many people fundamentally misunderstand what math is:

> Since arithmetic is what schools teach first, and since many people stop learning mathematics before they have progressed to anything else, it's not surprising that the words "mathematics" and "arithmetic" are often taken to be synonymous. But in fact, the more advanced parts of mathe-

matics have little to do with arithmetic . . . Indeed, some of the best mathematicians are not very good with figures.[6]

In order to see math the way mathematicians see it—as "the science of patterns"[7]—we need time to explore and uncover the subject (as suggested in the previous chapter). Moving beyond what has historically been taught first also allows us to help children develop a strong number sense, which many mathematicians agree is foundational for higher-level work. Number sense can be described as an ability to think about numbers in flexible and conceptual ways, including mental computation, visualizing numbers, connecting numbers to everyday problems, seeing relationships between numbers and groups of numbers, comparing numbers, and taking numbers apart in different ways.

Interviewed for an article in *The Atlantic* titled "5-Year-Olds Can Learn Calculus," "pioneering math educator and curriculum designer" Maria Droujkova concurs, saying that the traditional educational progression from arithmetic to algebra to geometry and so on "has nothing to do with how people think, how children grow and learn, or how mathematics is built."[8] Droujkova explains that there are different "levels of understanding" within the material, which the journalist summarizes like this: "After the informal level comes the level where students discuss ideas and notice patterns. Then comes the formal level, where students can use abstract words, graphs, and formulas. But ideally, a playful aspect is retained along the entire journey."[9]

In other words, understanding a discipline's scope is helpful but shouldn't pigeonhole us into how we explore it or how we should expect it to naturally unfold across a continuum. Proficiency can always change as new insights are gained. Even basic ideas can be explored more deeply with time. These levels of understanding don't always coincide with one another across every topic covered in the scope, and there's no need to expect formal understanding right from the start.

When we are only looking for a unitary understanding of facts in incremental doses rather than a network of knowledge that emerges over time, we reduce our repertoire for how we engage children to something that's dull and uninteresting.

In her book *Education and Learning to Think*, educational psychologist and professor Lauren Resnick writes about the assumption that thinking skills could be categorized into "higher order" and "lower order": "This assumption—that there is a sequence from lower level activities that do not require much independent thinking or judgment to higher level ones that do—colors much educational theory and practice. Implicitly at least, it justifies long years of drill on the 'basics' before thinking and problem solving are demanded."[10]

Seeing subjects across a continuum means doing the opposite of that. A continuum is a continuous sequence, something that keeps going but changes slightly in different ways. It is a range whose many parts contribute to a whole. An element of exploring how growth happens over time is taking our traditional understanding of how learning sequences for particular subjects and courses are formulated and holding them lightly. Conventional organization of how learning *should* happen is not a rigid truth that all educators even agree on; from country to country and even school to school, we find differences in the scope and sequence of various subjects. But by seeing subjects across a continuum, we can take time to allow our children to develop naturally, not in lockstep with a prescriptive application of education.

The Descriptive Lens

Now that we've reevaluated how we think about educational progression, let's move on to different tools we can use to help give a more complete picture of a child's development. The first is what I call the descriptive lens.

When we use concrete, descriptive language to report something, we paint a vivid, detailed picture of it with words. We show the qualities that something has without necessarily making a value judgment that restricts how the image's meaning is interpreted. We can use the descriptive lens as a filter through which we can observe our children at different moments in time, creating small additions to a larger, more comprehensive view of them in process—constantly evolving, never static, and so much more than what we imagine them to be. A lens like this gives us insight into how we might want to help further their growth. And at times when we do assign meaning to what we're describing, descriptive language can help us to at least recognize that we are doing so and reflect on the implications that it has for both us and the child or the child's work.

In the world of education, "descriptive inquiry" is a process based on closely observing someone or something, recording what you observe, and describing it with nonjudgmental language. It has largely been shaped by a collection of processes developed by the Prospect Center for Education and Research in North Bennington, Vermont, such as the Descriptive Review of the Child and the Descriptive Review of Work (among others). Each process has a different focus and purpose, but the foundation is the same for each one—education staff collaborating around open-ended questions that lead to true inquiry and the sense of possibility that accompanies it.

In particular, the process called Descriptive Review of the Child was designed to help teachers and parents pay attention to *how* a child learns rather than simply evaluating what they know, how they perform, or what they can do. "It is meant to give you, the important grown-ups in a child's life, a way to recognize fully how much you already know and understand. It is meant, too, to expand those understandings and to create a context of memory, ever growing and deepening, that will inform your own responses to children as individuals."[11] However, note that "the purpose of attending isn't to scrutinize children or even to 'figure them out'—and certainly not to change them into someone else. The purpose is simpler and more ordinary: to be more sensitively attuned to who they are and are becoming, so that, recognizing them as persons, we can assist and support their learning better."[12]

Teachers use a descriptive lens to do things like learn more about a child's values or better understand a special ability or talent they have. When they're worried about a child's progress, or when they have questions about a child's development, they can also rely on a descriptive stance first. It's a way of looking at children that attempts to see them holistically and understand them in novel ways.

My own educational work with children in schools was shaped by these processes. I came to value and support these practices and participated often in these kinds of reviews. So when I began homeschooling my children, I drew upon those experiences to help me frame and gain perspective about what I was noticing with my own children.

Throughout the years, I've relied on a descriptive lens to help me gain insight into all kinds of homeschooling questions. I've wondered how I could build a stronger connection with a particular child. I've asked myself how I could better "see" a more invisible, quieter child. I've questioned what interests or excites a particular child and what materials fire their creativity. I've asked myself whether I'm making too much of a child's disinterest in a particular subject or topic. I've deeply considered how to support a child who is struggling. I've deliberated about whether it's enough that a child happily complies with what I ask him to do. I've pondered the "what next" and asked, "Is there more?"

I've learned that I often need to take a step back from a situation in which I'm heavily involved or deeply invested so that I can see it with fresh eyes. Description helps me to see through a less tainted filter. To be clear, it's not a filter that's maliciously tainted. We all have a filter created by our values, experiences, biases, and beliefs through which we pass all of life's details. However, when we attempt to describe what we observe about our children with rich examples and illustrations in an anecdotal account, rather than immediately interpret it, we allow time and space for new, important information to emerge.

The following guidelines for painting a fuller picture of your child are derived from the Prospect Center's Descriptive Review of the Child, with my own interpretations and additions.[13] They are organized under categories to consider as you observe and reflect. The questions under each category are meant to help organize your thoughts; they're not an exhaustive list of all that can be considered. You might find that some headings or questions don't relate to you or that you need to add others.

As you go through them, it's important to try to ground your description in lots of narrative examples. I wouldn't necessarily attack every single question all at once, nor would I try to do this for each of my children at the same time. Sometimes I focus on one area or category and then choose a different one the next time. The idea is that, over time, you're building a layered narrative account of your child and your child's work. You can use this exercise to the extent that it adds to those layers and helps you to appreciate the richness revealed.

There's no appropriate number of times you should do this for each child. A few details recorded every week or every few days might be doable, but also, maybe it isn't. Doing it monthly might be too big of an undertaking, or it might seem like a reasonable goal. Perhaps doing it every few months or even once or twice a year could add something rich to how you see your child over time. At the very least, it can be quite a transformative experience to revisit what you've recorded and look for patterns that emerge (in what you notice, in your thinking, in your questions, and so on). I've never done this and regretted it. Even without the collaboration and multiple perspectives added by doing a formal review in an educational setting, the practice is powerful. I've even prepared formal reviews with parents who have said that just the process of preparing (going through the categories and answering the questions) yielded more than they expected.

Physical Presence and Gestures

What are some things that stand out to you about your child's physical presence? What is their size and build? How do they like to dress and wear their hair? How do they move through space and at what speed? When does that change? Are there gestures they make that characterize them? What kind of space do they like to occupy? Where and how do they like to position themselves? How do they move through indoor spaces and outdoor spaces? What activities do they like to do, and what kind of physical energy and gestures do they bring to these activities? When does your child seem most at ease and most uncomfortable, and what makes you able to determine the difference? Describe your child's voice and ways of speaking. What other physical ways do they express themselves? How easy is it to read the feelings your child is trying to express?

Disposition and Temperament

What is your child's temperament? What attitudes does your child typically show when it comes to the day-to-day goings-on of life? What is the range of emotions your child might experience in a day? What happens when circumstances change? What kinds of emotions are they comfortable displaying? What kind of emotion makes them uncomfortable? What stirs deep feelings for your child? What are their deep commitments and personal loyalties? What happens when those loyalties are threatened? What goes against their sense of honor? What is their idea of justice? How do they express it?

Connections with Other People

Think about your child in the company of others. What kind of place do they create for themselves in familiar settings? How do they accomplish this? How do they respond to those who are unfamiliar? What do they do around new people or new groups of children? What role do they assume in close friendships or sibling relationships? Who are they drawn to? How do they act among more casual acquaintances? How do they engage in group games and activities? When arguments happen or when tension arises, how does your child respond? When do they withdraw from the group or family? How do they withdraw?

Do they respond differently to adults than they do to other children? What adults are they drawn to, and what draws them? What adults do they avoid and why? How does your child greet familiar people? What kind of response does your child expect from you? From other adults? From friends? From siblings? What makes your child feel valued, loved, supported, and safe? How do others (adults and children) respond to your child? How easily do others recognize and value them? What makes it easy? What makes it difficult? What kinds of adult responses earn the child's respect, and what kind lead to anger, frustration, or disappointment?

Strong Interests and Preferences

Make a list of all the things your child likes. Include food, movies, games, books, places, people, etc. Also make a list of all that your child dislikes. Are there patterns that emerge between both lists? How often do these lists change? What has endured? How do they express their likes and dislikes? What questions have lingered in your child's mind? What are they curious about? What have they been persistent about knowing? Is it a range of things? Do these things tend to fall under a particular category, or are they wildly different? How does your child express their interests in play, games, movies, books, and other activities? What kind of play or media captivates them?

What would they choose to do given unlimited time and resources? Lists of "favorite things" can also be helpful—favorite books, movies, shows, songs, and so on, especially if patterns and range are also considered. Are there particular topics or themes your child likes to explore in play (like superheroes, ninjas, animals, or families)? What rules are there? What makes the play go right? What makes it go wrong? What do other children have to be able to do to join in? What role do they like to assume in sustaining the play?

Modes of Thinking and Learning

This category is meant to consider how your child thinks about and approaches the world. Stemming directly from their strong interests, their modes of thinking and learning lend insight into the ways they create knowledge. What kinds of things does your child intuitively know? What kinds of activities or ideas do they have an aptitude for? When and how are you able to observe it? Does your child think their ability is special, or are they unaware of it?

What subjects is your child drawn to and why? What *aren't* they drawn to and why? How does your child work through problems? How do they go about figuring things out? How do they try to find answers to things they want to know? Do they use their hands or bodies to inform their thoughts? Do they quietly observe? Do they notice and tend to remember? Do they dismantle objects or ideas to reconstruct them? Do they organize scattered parts? Do they research? How? Under what circumstances do they prefer one approach over another?

Are they inclined toward mathematical, poetic, philosophical, or any other types of thinking? It's important to remember the Reggio Emilia concept that children have "one hundred languages" and that they all express themselves in different ways at different times. A proclivity toward one should not mandate that others be ignored. We are complex people and cannot be categorically put into a box without allowing room to be more than the box determines.

Now think about your child as they learn a specific skill. How do they approach the new task? Are they hesitant? Enthusiastic? Independent? Stressed? Do they take their time? What do they do with that time? If they ask for help, what kind of help do they ask for? Do they like to work alone or alongside others? Does all this change when the skill being learned is one that they have chosen themselves? That might add some nuance to how you see your child as a learner.

What does your child do when they encounter problems or mistakes in their work? How do they handle interruptions? Competitive situations? What kinds of standards does your child have for themselves in their work? What makes them proud? What makes them want to redo or rework something? How do you know? How does your child reveal their values? What influences your child's standards? Do standards change when the work is their choice? Do your expectations for your child influence how they assess themselves? Is there a conflict between the two? How might your child's interests be deepened or expanded? How might you support them and give them opportunities to sustain their work?

Collections of Work

In schools that engage in the type of Descriptive Inquiry explained above, it is common to see a similar effort to glean insight from not only the child but also the child's work. When I was a teacher, the school facilitated this by having teachers keep collections of a variety of examples of each child's work right inside the classroom. The collections followed the child throughout the grades. However, I have adapted the practice for use at home, so I'll describe it with that in mind.

Patricia Carini, who was instrumental in developing the descriptive processes, suggested this work could include "anything a child made, constructed, wrote, including, but not limited to, the following: drawings; paintings; collage; sculpture; sewing; block, wood, Lego and junk constructions; photographs and films; stories, poems, reports, essays, the occasional novel, and informational writing."[14] Because we often see our children (especially young ones) drawing motifs like houses or familiar people repeatedly, we might question whether there's value in adding multiple examples of this kind of work to the collection. But interestingly, if we look at these drawings, it's unlikely that they will be identical; the differences might even be something to be explored.

Many homeschoolers have a similar practice of keeping a "portfolio," but there is a key difference: traditional portfolios are designed to be evaluated by someone on the outside, while a collection of work is created primarily for the child and the child's family. It is intended to help the child look at their work over time in a visual way, reflect on their process and their growth, generate new ideas for their future work, and share about themselves and their work with the rest of the family.

The collections demonstrate the process of learning just as much as they show an end product. That's because, more than a selection of highly polished work, a collection is a showcase of the diversity of interests and features that define the work. This variety can help show the extent of just how much a person has grown.

A collection of work is not simply meant to be a place where work is stored and then forgotten. It's an interactive part of the learning experience that is reviewed periodically or as often as the child would like. (In fact, it's helpful to have collections of work on hand when a child is writing or dictating a self-reflection, which I'll discuss in the next section.)

Collections grow and change as the child grows and changes, developing gradually and progressively right alongside them. At home, a collection of work could be a physical collection of anything a child makes or does, placed inside a bin or large folder, or it could be a digital folder of written work, photographs, videos, or other media. Whatever it is or however you store it, use it as part of your ongoing work.

When my daughter was younger, we once pulled out her collection to see if it would spark some ideas for a new project. After looking through a whole stack of paintings, she noticed how she enjoyed painting a lot of nature scenes. After a moment, her eyes lit up, and she remembered that she wanted to know a whole lot more about birds. To her surprise, the next day, her dad discovered a bird's nest in the potted plant right outside our front door. From that point on, I would say that all my children embarked on a study of birds that went on for months. In that time, they set up bird feeders, went bird-watching, kept birding journals, wrote bird stories, built a birdhouse with wood and tools, sculpted clay birds, made bird drawings and paintings, created a bird game, wrote a bird-call songbook, and much more.

Slowly they became more and more knowledgeable about birds. Their interests were developing over time, and time was precisely what they needed to be able to explore and revisit their interests and ideas often. You will even see later, in the section on documentation, that I noticed this interest a whole year before they began this intense study. Our collection of my daughter's work was key to how this experience unfolded.

What I love about collections of work is that they make it easy to celebrate how far the child has come, not just how far they have still to go to reach some ideal that isn't even their own. While we can spend a lot of time preoccupied with the shortfalls we see, collections of work help us celebrate the gains.

Self-Reflections

A self-reflection is when a child looks back over their past work, notices their growth over time, and reflects on their learning. We do these at the end of every year and periodically throughout the year. The end-of-the-year reflections tend to cover a lot of different areas, but we also use the process for reflecting on one abiding interest, looking at development in one single subject or with one goal in mind.

These reflections can be done in writing or orally. Children who are not comfortable writing on their own have dictated their thoughts to me, and together, over a few days, we've gone over their words, revising and adding details when necessary. It is always a good idea to have the work you're reflecting on right in front of you. Pull it out of the digital file or physical collection, and record the child's thoughts as they look over their work. Ask them questions about what they notice to help them extract more from their thinking. Ask them if they notice any patterns or themes that emerge in their thinking or in their work.

I thought it might be helpful to see an example of a self-reflection, and my daughter permitted me to share a portion of hers with you. She was specifically focusing on her development in writing fiction stories:

> *Over time, I've noticed that rather than writing once upon a time stories I'm able to write more complex, dramatic stories that pull people in so that they want to keep reading. I've also noticed that more and more I'm enjoying writing very action-packed scenes, with a lot of mystery throughout the story in general. I notice that what comes easy to me now is setting the scene. I can easily paint a picture for the reader to imagine.*
>
> *One thing that I will say has stayed the same for me is that I can never finish a story that I begin. I always write these exciting starters but never seem to be able to move on past the "big bang" beginning. There are some parts of doing this that are challenging, and other parts that are not. After I've written one really good thing, I get another really good idea for a different story that I feel like I have to write down too.*
>
> *In [a certain piece of writing], I was trying to write a scene that pulled the reader in and held them captive in a world that I created out of pure imagination. I wanted to really hook my reader and paint a picture for them inside their heads that would inspire them.*
>
> *The beginning of this particular story is really rushed and holds a lot of keys to the unfolding drama, so I had to clearly*

write in a way that the reader would know exactly what was happening. I added some description, but not too much. Just the right amount so you can get the gist of the storyline.

In the fight scene, there are two characters that are communicating only a little. There are sentences of dialogue that are short and quick like punches and then others that are longer and dramatic where I showed the goriness of the damage done in the scene.

The background is really important. People in the crowd say key things. Someone who will play a major part later in the story comes in and ends the scene. That part moves a little slower but still makes you hold your breath. It leaves some mystery. Everything isn't revealed about their punishment and whether they'll be okay. With this story, I'm still working on the cool down after the "big bang" of a beginning. For me, it seems a little bland for my taste.

I want to point out that in her self-reflection, my daughter was telling us how she wants her work to be read. She told us what she was trying to do and achieve. Essentially, she told us how she developed her work to her own standards. Without her voice, it might not have been obvious how she had been trying to refine her writing over time. With her reflection, the picture of her growth is much more dimensional than if I was only evaluating the writing by my own checks and measures (e.g., paragraph form, compelling title, correctly punctuated dialogue, opening hook, etc.). Sometimes growth and learning mean more to the child than simply accomplishing what we think we were "teaching."

Documenting Work

We use documentation as a way of recording or keeping track of the process of ongoing work, specifically work that is self-directed. I document things I notice about my children and their work, and my children also do their own documentation of their personal work. Since this is not something that happened overnight, I want to first begin by explaining to you how the foundation of my children noticing, describing, and thinking about their thinking was built.

I gave lots of examples of how our Project Time works in chapter 6. About twice a week at the end of our work times, we naturally come together to share our work. Usually, one person will talk and then afterward, the others are invited to make comments and ask questions. Before doing this, we spend time discussing the kinds of things you could notice about someone's work and talking with descriptive language, so that there's an expectation that their comments and questions are both respectful and helpful. No matter how each child chooses to spend their time each day, I want to highlight and show that what they do is important and that it is valued by the entire family. I want us to see each other through the work that we do.

On other days, my children spend time documenting their work: taking pictures, writing notes, and reflecting on how things went. Before this routine started, we talked about what documentation is and what people use it for. Artists like Leonardo da Vinci and Frida Kahlo, for example, created sketchbooks and kept diaries. Scientists record their data all the time. People keep all kinds of lists, tallies, and notes for a variety of reasons. We talked about why and discussed how documentation looks different depending on what you're working on.

My children also use documentation to be observers of themselves. For a younger child, documentation might look like: describing their work to another person and telling the story of how they created it; a question-and-answer session with others about the work; drawing a picture that shows their process, plans, or product (what they're doing or making); coming up with interview questions they plan to use; voicing observations they make while studying something; coming up with a list of things they want to remember from a book they look through; generating words they want to put with something they have drawn. Many of these examples can be accomplished with the help of an adult or with the adult acting as a scribe.

For an older child, documentation might include photos or video footage of their process with notes to keep it organized; journal entries that keep track of questions they have along the way, materials they've used, what is going well, what is difficult, problems they've had and what they did to try to solve them, or what they might do tomorrow; notes from a topic they're researching; and drawings, sketches, charts, graphs, or lists that might be relevant.

Also foundational was the time we spent generating a list of "What's important to record?" I worked with my children, prompting them to come up with a list of the kinds of things they could document about their work. We talked through this repeatedly. On their list are things like: your feelings about your work, what you'll do the next day, your questions, how you think your work could be better, what went well, and what didn't go well.

To make the whole documentation process easier, we use dedicated Project Time journals and digital portfolio apps. With these apps, they can take photographs and videos of their work, write notes, and add voice recordings (which is great for non-readers and -writers). They can also view each other's work and make comments. I make it a little more interactive by responding to things they've recorded and saying, "Tell me more about this," or "What do you plan to do about this?" I sometimes give feedback or make suggestions about things they could try.

I keep a journal as well. I use it as a tool for noticing and remembering. I write down what I'm observing about their work, their play, and their choices. By writing it down, I can revisit my thinking and then mentor them toward furthering their work. Sometimes my journal is full of lists reminding me to do things like buy more glue sticks, but it's also a place to safely write down my ideas. I write down all the resources I'd pull in or related activities I might attempt if I was the one directing the work. Having my journal as a dumping ground for my thoughts helps me resist the urge to derail whatever they're doing. And even when I make suggestions along the way, I don't get offended if my children don't use them.

Here's an example of an entry from my journal made a whole year before the start of the intense bird study I referenced earlier:

We went for our usual walk this afternoon. My daughter and oldest son were both on their bikes and I was pushing the babies in the stroller. At one point my daughter was up ahead and pulled over at the side of the lake beckoning her brother to hurry and check out what she had found. There on the ground were two extremely large feathers. She was amazed saying that she had never seen feathers that big before. She held one and he held the other and they pretended to flap their wings and flutter around like birds. After a little while, they politely traded feathers with each other and fluttered around again. She hypothesized that these feathers were from hawks. We had just seen, moments before, some hawks flying overhead. When my son exclaimed, "Look at the eagles!" she quickly corrected him saying that they were hawks. I asked how she knew that they were hawks, and she began to describe things she noticed about them. She asked me if I thought the feathers were from a hawk, and we talked about the kind of research we could do to find out. She asked if we were being paleontologists. That led to a wonderful discussion of words and ornithology. My son practiced saying or-ni-thol-o-gy really slowly as we talked. He wondered out loud if hawks had teeth. Elated about their find, our discussion turned toward how and why feathers were used for pens. They asked if it was possible to try to write with the feathers they found. That led to another discussion about the Migratory Bird Treaty Act. Wow, what a day!

The journal is a place for my thoughts about my children's interests, no matter where those interests are occurring. I also have journals in which I document my personal work that I share with my children. It serves a dual purpose of modeling for them the act of reflecting and recording. After my brother died, I kept a sketchbook in which I would document my process of learning to draw some very specific subjects. In it, I also recorded my feelings and thoughts about my work. My brother was an artist, and drawing and journaling helped me in some ways to feel more connected to him. The result was powerful, not because I had beautiful sketches to frame and display, but because of how much I also learned about myself in the process.

I want to emphasize that we did not add in all these documentation routines at once. We built them slowly over time. We focused on one thing until we got good at it, or until I understood it better, and then attempted to tackle more. These things take time.

I also want to point out that documentation is not a mandatory element for doing self-directed work—it's a companion practice that works nicely to help look at growth over time. Please don't think that if you're not doing it then you are doing Project Time or any other kind of self-directed learning "wrong." (You'll remember me saying in chapter 6 that there is no one correct way to do it.)

If you think that adding documentation to a self-directed work routine would generate a negative response from your children, note that you can actually document most of it yourself with a quick photo and a couple of sentences about their response to a question you ask them. Your objective isn't to force them to add an extra component to their self-directed work. That said, many children will want to document their work in some way, especially as they get older, because they'll see a real need for it; that's why it's important to lay the groundwork by helping them understand the ways people use documentation in the real world.

Recognizing Learning outside of Conventional Work

One of the reasons the documentation described in the previous section is helpful is that it can help us notice growth when our children are doing so much learning but aren't always producing conventional work. We can capture, through narrative snapshots or digital media, things that we observe about our children along the way, rather than just an evaluation of an end result.

Why is this important? Right off the bat, I would say that just because learning is invisible to us doesn't mean that it's absent or unsubstantial. I tell myself often that I don't need to know every detail of what my children have learned to trust that they have truly learned. My understanding is irrelevant. My inability to name it does not negate its existence.

Second, I think it's important to value the process of building knowledge over producing the "right answer." Progress trumps perfection any day of the week. This is why documenting the process becomes important—you can go back to it to remind yourself of all that was involved. I know it can be hard to capture the expanse of a child's imagination. Those are the moments born of questions, thoughts, observations, and experiments. That's why we document the messy, the imperfect, and the unfinished, even if there's nothing pretty to show for it at the end. The evidence of learning is all around us. It's in the in-between.

Third, I think it's important to be attentive to the intention behind what our children are doing. Why would we value something they create without also seeing value in what they decide to do with that creation? Would you create a tool and then never use it? Cook a meal and then never eat it? Build a world and then not play in it? Sometimes there is fulfillment in the creative process alone. It's why a sculptor can mold something and then smash it, or a painter can joyfully produce a painting that sits in a drawer indefinitely. But sometimes, creativity yields a desire for use, or a purpose that transcends the need to create.

Sometimes our children will want their creation to send a message that we don't understand. Or they might try to connect their work to a larger issue or event of their choosing. Perhaps they may want to use what they create as a way of seeking adventure or entertainment. No matter the purpose, I believe we must respect the maker's intention. It's just as valuable as their hands being "busy." Sometimes the busyness of the hands and the production of something visible are the only aspects of our children's work that we are comfortable with, because it comes closest to the conventional proof of learning—the kind that falls inside normative school-based parameters. But we need to permit ourselves to explore differently. A maker's intent might be a worthy one, even if it exists outside of our comfort zone. Being attentive to the intention can reveal layers of understanding, intellectual energy, and meaning deeper than what can be seen in just the work itself.

Lastly, recognizing the learning is also about realizing that we might be holding the work to the wrong standards. A child's own standards for their work are just as important as another person's standards for the child's work (if not more). When we worry that they won't have their own intrinsic motivation, we push our parameters, limits, and goals upon them, but that is not the only way to get them to learn.

Now, what about when you must translate the learning you now recognize (no matter what form it takes) back to traditional ways of reporting progress? Your observations and notes on what you've noticed about your children over time will be useful to you as you continue to support them and their development. However, you may worry about how this translates to the kind of traditional progress reporting that the academic world outside of your home values, or maybe you need to report to educational authorities in the place where you homeschool.

The fancy language such authorities use to describe skills might impress you, but don't let it intimidate you into believing that your learning doesn't measure up. Here's an example of showing educational value in what, to many, would just look like play. For a few weeks, my son took an interest in battling his Beyblades (spinning tops made of metal or plastic pieces that you combine and launch for optimal effect). He liked predicting which ones would win based on factors like weight and speed, and he explored many physics concepts as he set up each battle. I could have easily said, "Really? That's what you want to do with your Project Time?" But instead, I took his plan and validated it by giving him the time and space to do it. I was saying, implicitly, "This is good work because it's your work." In the process, here's what he accomplished:

- Graph making
- Experimenting
- Record keeping
- Writing an instruction manual including tips and tricks
- Pinpointing the variables in testing and coming up with controls
- Figuring out how torque and weight affect precession
- Exploring angular velocity and spin angles
- Learning how friction and force affect velocity
- Discovering how recoil is a factor when the Beyblades are battling
- Discussing how the weight of the Beyblade and diameter of the whorl affect how long it spins

See? You can speak the same fancy language if you so choose or if it's required for reporting progress to your local governing body. You simply link the skills they're highlighting to what you see in your children's work, even when they're exploring and practicing them in unconventional ways. More importantly, you'll know how to stay attentive to the things you value, how to respond thoughtfully to the things you notice, and how to practice patience and compassion as you support your growing children.

Charts, Checklists, and Logs

Charts, checklists, logs, and the like are the final tools I'd like to mention. We can use them to create a school record by collecting and organizing bits of data little by little as the learning experiences happen, so that all together, over time, they tell a story of how learning has continued. We can use them to keep track of projects our children have worked on, books our children have read, places we have visited, the time they've spent on various activities, writing skills they've been working on, or math concepts they've explored.

You can monitor this data with the type of charts, checklists, and logs that are made for the specific purpose of offering feedback and showing a child's progress. These usually include criteria to keep track of and a range of responses to each one, such as "Not yet/ Revisit," "Still developing/Needs support," and "Consistent/Works independently." When you look back at these tools over time, you can visibly see your child's growth. You can sometimes find these kinds of charts in the instructor materials of a curriculum that you use. Don't be afraid to edit them to suit your purposes, especially if they don't help you see your children with the type of span you're looking for. Alternatively, you can create your own to reflect the benchmarks that you find valuable.

When I was a classroom teacher, we sometimes used these kinds of tools to accompany our narrative-style reports, which, by contrast, were full of colorful descriptions and rich anecdotal details. Parents gave feedback that having both the checklists and the narrative reports helped them to make sense of all the information we were sending out. I'm not entirely sure how useful these checklists would have been to them on their own without the other specifics, but in a home setting, where you're the one observing, keeping notes, following progress, and constantly reflecting on how things are going, they might serve a great purpose.

As with any other tool for tracking progress over time, allow the insight you gain from these activities to impact you and influence the ways that you extend, enhance, refine, and return to the work in question. All the tools described in this chapter are authentic, valid ways of knowing, for you and your child, and they can be an active, dynamic resource for continued learning and growth.

PART THREE

The Bigger Picture and the Wider World

CHAPTER 9

Connection through Relationship

Strengthening the Parent-Child Bond

You are on this journey together for the rest of your life, so keep moving forward together, making memories, and having adventures and trust that the heart connections are being made slowly but surely.

—GRETA ESKRIDGE, *ADVENTURING TOGETHER*

Education is so much more than simply learning facts. It depends heavily on the relationship between the invested parties. Its transformative power is nestled inside every exchange, whether between parent and child, teacher and student, mentor and mentee, trainer and apprentice, team members, collaborators, partners, or friends. In that relationship, there is potential to grow beyond your own perspective and understanding. Education lives by listening, dialogue, and participation with others in all kinds of encounters. It thrives where there is mutual respect. The relationship, to me, is everything.

At home with our children, the relational dynamic is yet more compelling. Our children aren't just looking for information from us—they're looking for love. They want us to lead with hearts that genuinely love them. One simple way to define love is as a deep and meaningful sense of belonging and connection. We as parents can create a strong bond with our children. Deep and meaningful connection is something we have the privilege of building. So why not put it at the forefront of our homeschooling experience? To make the most of the time we have with our children is to cultivate that connection at every stage of their growth.

Slow schooling affords us opportunities to grow our relationships with our children. In her book *The Lifegiving Home*, Sally Clarkson tells us that "all relationships grow in proportion to the investment of time and individual attention that has been put into them."[1] Learners flourish in an environment where they can peacefully pursue meaningful work and we can work alongside them, making space to be attentive to their educational needs. We can partner with our children in ways that build trust and maintain healthy attachments.

The "Family Dinner" of Education

I don't know a lot of people who cry at cooking-oriented TV shows like *Family Dinner* or *Somebody Feed Phil*, but I definitely have. I'm so moved by the ways that food brings people together, becoming a point of connection. That connection is why eating dinner with one's family can be such a powerful ritual. Kim John Payne writes in *Simplicity Parenting*:

> The family dinner is more than a meal. Coming together, committing to a shared time and experience, exchanging conversation, food, and attention . . . all of these add up to more than full bellies. The nourishment is exponential. Family stories, cultural markers, and information about how we live are passed around with the peas. The process is more than the meal: It is what comes before and after. It is the reverence paid. The process is also more important than the particulars. Not only is it more forgiving, but also, like any rhythm, it gets better with practice.[2]

I see slow schooling as the "family dinner" of education. It unifies the family because of what it is and what it stands for. It is more than education. The partnership and connection around a shared experience add up to something far greater. The growth for everyone (including parents) is immense. The process is what defines it. It's what gets you to the learning, what keeps you muddling around inside of it, and what brings you through to the other side of it.

One family's particulars will look different from another's, but the process is the whole point. When everyone is responsible for creating it, all are invested in the outcome. The process weaves in the ups and downs, the successes and failures, and creates closeness between its participants. When we prioritize relationships, we stay committed to the process. But more than that, we stay committed to one another. In the preparation, the practice, and the procedures, we build connection and get to enjoy something that will nourish the entire family.

Layers of Connection

In chapter 4, I mentioned my affection for the Japanese painting style called Nihonga. It has been called "slow art" because of the time it takes to prepare the paint, the meticulous way it gets painted in layers, and the way it's meant to be observed. The artist gains a deep intimacy with the work through the time they spend with it, and anyone experiencing the art can also know the work better the longer they allow themselves to really look at it. I see slow schooling as a slow art, and again, at the heart of it, is relationship. The longer we remain engaged, the better we know the process, ourselves, and each other.

At the end of it all, my children and I should be more bonded, not less; our hearts closer, not farther apart; our interactions warmer, not cooler; our connection deeper, not more superficial. From their youngest years, through layered interactions of mind, body, and heart, we practice relating to our children inside the varied, brilliant, multifaceted experience of the slow art itself. We are "painting" this work with our best materials. Even if we have inadvertently built patterns of relating that give us frustrating outcomes and aren't sustainable in the long run, we can always begin to broaden our repertoire of connection-based hues. I once heard Pam Leo, author of *Connection Parenting*, say that "our greatest power as parents is our power to choose. We will either repeat or evolve."[3] We don't have to remain stuck in the same undesirable place, devoid of closeness throughout our entire school experience.

So let's explore for a moment the idea of layered interaction. How can we use it to relate to our children better?

- Mind-to-mind connection is the free-flowing exchange of ideas. It often occurs through conversations that generate exciting and interesting mental energy. It happens easily around shared interests or whenever two people can share their thoughts or engage in joint challenges of the intellect.

- Body-to-body connection happens through physical touch. We tend to think only in terms of physical moments like hugs and kisses, but it's also smaller points of contact like touching an arm or patting a back or even nonphysical contact such as looking someone in the eye. It can even be engaging in physical activity like sports or games together.

- Heart-to-heart connection is the free-flowing exchange of emotions. That doesn't always mean tears or screaming and yelling (two extremes on the emotional spectrum). It's baring your heart and communicating in a way that matches the vulnerability of the other person.

By intentionally creating connection with all these methods in mind, we can improve the bond that we forge with our children. Whenever I closely inspect the time I spend with my children and how we interact, I notice things I could improve. The first time I did this, I noticed that I tended to think very generally about my parenting. *In general*, I knew we were doing okay with connection. But a close inspection brought a new level of awareness and allowed me to make small efforts throughout the day that were much more deliberate. It was the impetus behind the Connection Calendar I created (available on my website), which operates on the premise that one step at a time, through the accumulation of many small interactions, we love and remain willing to grow. Just as slow art requires an investment of time, so does the strength of the family bond.

Authenticity in Connection

An authentic connection is one that isn't obstructed or hindered by disruptors like guilt over failed expectations, a desire to control birthed out of fear, or other distractions. When we create an environment in which our children *can't* show up authentically, we're adding to conditions that subtly disrupt what we are building.

When my boys were young, I sat down with them one day to do some math work. We began by reviewing some of the concepts we had explored earlier in the week. I started noticing that whatever questions I asked them as part of the review, they gave silly, intentionally wrong answers to try to cover up the fact that they didn't know or didn't remember whatever I was asking them.

My response wasn't the best. I scolded them about not knowing and probably made them feel embarrassed about it as well. Thankfully, I caught myself and realized that in just a few short years of their lives, I had expected them, after hearing this information only one or two times, to completely understand it, understand the why behind it, retain it, and regurgitate it too. They couldn't just show up in that moment however they were truly feeling—a little lost and fuzzy on the details—because I was demanding that they operate in a box that I had created for them. Through my reaction, I was demonstrating that I valued performative cooperation over authentic exchange. A lack of authenticity will cause our children to hide more and more pieces of themselves over time to please us.

Guilt is another element with similar consequences that disrupts connection. We feel guilt when we think we messed up, did something wrong, or even just didn't meet expectations.

Has your child ever excitedly brought you something they've written, like a story or letter, and instead of sharing their joy in what they wrote, you automatically look at the misspellings and punctuation errors? Your face, body language, and possibly your words aren't exactly the reaction your child is hoping for. Their excitement immediately turns to disappointment when they realize that they've somehow made you unhappy. They thought they'd done something amazing, but they were met with disapproval. They feel guilty about not meeting your expectations, and before long, you feel guilty too, because it's yet another time that you responded in the wrong way. You end up feeling like you failed them. To make matters worse, your child will probably have some reservations the next time they want to share something with you. There won't be the same level of excitement.

That's just one example. I can think of others that, unfortunately, have created the same types of feelings, with the same kind of results. When these feelings build up between us and our children, it damages the authenticity of the connection. If we let guilt fester for too long, it changes the way we relate to one another altogether.

Getting in Sync

An absence of harmony in the home can be characterized by constant tension, broken relationship, and a loss of mutual respect and trust. Educating our children can seem far from the joyful experience we want it to be when we are constantly met with resistance. A lack of connection makes any attempts to parent seem like draconian directives in the wake of what child development authorities Gordon

Neufeld and Gabor Maté refer to as a child's "counterwill"[4] (their resistance to compulsion or pressure).

When parents resort to coercion and manipulation as leverage to get their children to do things, whether school-related or not, they're not relying on what Neufeld and Maté deem the true "source of our parenting power": connection itself.[5] "By cultivating the connection first," they write in *Hold On to Your Kids*, "we minimize the risk of resistance and lessen the chances of setting ourselves up for our own negative reactions. Whether with the uncooperative toddler or the recalcitrant adolescent, the parent first needs to draw near the child, reestablishing emotional closeness before expecting compliance."[6]

When met with resistance, it's natural to want to back off, and it's easy to pretend we don't care. But it's never too late to restore a broken connection, or to take steps toward getting back in sync with a child who seems emotionally far away. It might not happen overnight, but the effort is so worth it.

Calling our children into safety, from a place of disconnection to a place of connection, requires us to be mindful of our reactions (especially to resistance) and expectations. Sometimes we have expectations for our children that aren't even appropriate for who they are, their ages, or the stages that they're in. We must be intentional about managing our responses and course-correcting ourselves when necessary. We can't overcomplicate the way back to a close relationship. Dr. Laura Markham, the clinical psychologist who founded Aha! Parenting, has this to say on her blog:

> Often, we go whole days or even weeks just moving our kids through the schedule, without taking time to really connect. And most parents can't imagine where they would find more time to connect. So look for opportunities that are already in your schedule, where you can slow down and create an opportunity for closeness. . . . Intimacy is a dance. It deepens or is eroded by every interaction we have. The

good news? That means that every interaction you have is a chance to shift onto a positive track and deepen your connection to your loved ones. Just paying attention for a week to how you respond when your children reach out to you can shift the whole tone in your family.[7]

Slow schooling is replete with opportunities to cultivate meaningful connection. In fact, that can be one of the main objectives of slow schooling.

Connection vs. Control

A sense of control over what is happening in our homes correlates, parents believe, with a good outcome. But an element of our need to control can really be birthed out of fear. Uncertainty or fear about whatever we don't know makes us feel insecure (which is not good for any kind of connection), and sometimes control is our way of trying to jumpstart certainty and feel more confident in what we're doing.

Take routines, for example. When we work overtime trying to keep everything organized just right, getting everything done on our agenda, we will find ourselves doing so at the expense of connection. Interactions with our children can become strained because we're predominantly leading with control. I find that when I'm focused on controlling every moment of the day, I'm maximizing the importance of what I think needs to be controlled and minimizing my ability to be present and truly enjoy our time together. I miss out on opportunities to have fun with my children and to be more fulfilled as a parent. Instead, I magnify my own insecurities, fears, and doubts about so many underlying things, which manifests as a need to control *everything*.

We all want a more fruitful and fulfilling experience in our parenting. We don't just want our relationship with our children to produce the intended results; we want to enjoy it. Constant control might allow us to think we're getting things done, but it robs us of the fulfillment part. That's why there needs to be a balance. What characterizes our connection is that we take delight in raising our children and in the process of learning to form better bonds. That doesn't mean we're happy all day, every day. That's an unrealistic expectation. However, the moments of enjoying our children should be greater than the moments of not enjoying them.

Removing Distractions

I find that one of the biggest roadblocks to experiencing deep and meaningful connection is distraction. In general, distractions keep us from giving something our full attention, and because the responsibilities of being a parent are many, our attention can seem heavily divided. We can think of distractions as how we spend our time, energy, and attention when they're not aligned with our values. If we keep our true values in focus, we won't waste our efforts on things that rob us of a deeper level of closeness with our loved ones.

Even on days when family life feels hectic and I've hardly had any meaningful interactions with my children, I try to make it a priority to put down the phone, make lots of eye contact, get down to their level or in their physical space, and relate with them mind-to-mind, body-to-body, or heart-to-heart. Life stressors, big and small, don't always make this easy, but it's important for our children to have a strong family bond as they face challenges of their own.

Family consultant Kim John Payne refers to efforts like these as "strengthening the family base camp." He writes, "When life gets shaky for your child *out there*, in the world, it's important to make certain life *in here*, within the family sphere, is solid."[8] Our own challenges will require that we attend to our personal needs so that we can offer our best selves to our families. In a world where slow and intentional are not the norm, connection is an opportunity for everyone to be present and to silence the chaos.

Toni Morrison, Nobel laureate and novelist, on an episode of the *Oprah Winfrey Show* in 2000, talked about seeing our children:

It's interesting to see when a kid walks into the room . . . does your face light up? That's what they're looking for. When my children used to walk in the room when they were little, I looked at them to see if they had buckled their trousers, or if their hair was combed, or their socks were up . . . so you think your affection and your deep love is on display 'cause you're caring for them. It's not. When they see you they see the critical face . . . What's wrong now? But then if you let your . . . face speak what's in your heart . . . because when they walked in the room I was glad to see them. It's just as small as that, you see.[9]

Are we caught up with the daily responsibilities of raising children, the daily grind of homeschooling, thinking that our love is visible or obvious because of how hard we're working, when all the while, we've forgotten one of our children's greatest needs—connection? Do we truly see *them*, or do we only see what we have to do *for* them? And when we see them, do we smile?

Remember the Haven

Slow schooling just for the sake of learning has benefits, but embracing the process right alongside our children and growing together in relationship with them adds so much more. Pervasive societal messaging says that as children grow older, they simply grow apart from their parents, but strengthening our bonds with them is an intentional investment in something that matters greatly.

So much togetherness can be both a pitfall and a perk, but as with many of life's paradoxes, we can engage that tension for the purpose of growth. We don't always realize what's required to hold tension until we're out there feeling pulled in two opposite directions, but as we assimilate both realities and remain "in process," new things can and will emerge. Building a better connection with our children will pull things out of us that we didn't know were there—for the better. It's hard work, but dedication does have its rewards.

Our parenting, in all the ordinary, unglamorous moments, through time spent together with our children, should be an extension of the safety our homes represent. As Ainsley Arment puts it in her book *The Wild + Free Family,* "We're laying the foundation for a fortress that will withstand the harshest winds and the fiercest storms. We are building an estate of love that will serve as a safe haven for years to come."[10] Our children need us. Let's let slow schooling be the arena where meaningful connection is rehearsed over and over again.

CHAPTER 10

Connection to the Natural World

Balanced by the Outdoors

Our relationship with nature is not only about preserving land and water,
but about preserving and growing the bonds between us.

—RICHARD LOUV, *THE NATURE PRINCIPLE*

A few years ago, my children and I went for a hike in a local wilderness area that is a habitat for the American alligator. We were all crossing a huge log over a narrow body of algae-infested swamp water when one child slipped and fell in. A river otter suspiciously eyeballing the commotion seemed to be the only animal around, but our reactions were still swift. As we all struggled to stay balanced single file on the log, one child tried to pull up the child who had fallen and was now standing waist-deep in swamp water. Another child started yelling at the others to move aside so that I could more easily reach the child who fell. Yet another child was crying. In the end, we were able to get our rescuee safely back on the log, but now wet, muddy, and overwhelmed, he became fearful of crossing the rest of the way. He finally managed to get down on his belly and shimmy toward the bank on the other side.

Once the hike was over and we were back in our car, we debriefed about the events that unfolded. We realized we'd each responded very differently to the stressful situation. There were many tears shed as we talked through it all, and although it's difficult to explain, I felt so much closer to my children at that moment. I knew deep down that every negative thing we'd gone through had unexpectedly cultivated meaningful connection among us. As homeschool mom Greta Eskridge writes, "That is the magic of misadventure. The hardships and the struggle, the scary parts, even the undesirable parts all create this special bond that happens faster and holds stronger than the bonds made in our regular, humdrum days."[1]

Nature adventures like these have a knack for strengthening everyone's bonds as they experience new things together. However, nature also provides so much more. You don't even have to be a nature enthusiast to benefit from the balance that it brings. If we dare to view the natural world as a necessary component of how we see and use time, especially as it relates to slow schooling, we can begin to encounter some significant things.

A Sense of Place

In his book *How to Raise a Wild Child*, science communicator Scott Sampson writes, "In the end, to be connected to nature is to expand one's awareness and become native to place."[2] Borrowing from thinkers like environmental activist and writer Wendell Berry, Sampson shows how knowledge about one's close natural environment can be the forerunner for the kinds of knowing that inform a great many different domains. "Knowledge is at its best when it passes through our heads *and* our hearts," he writes. "A strong sense of place rooted in emotional connection reveals the beauty of the natural world, the truth of our embeddedness within nature, and the goodness inherent in caring for one's home ground."[3]

Engaging children (and ourselves) in nature through consistent, gradually intensive experiences helps develop an understanding of the

interconnectedness of our world. Being truly "embedded within nature" (engaging with it, noticing it, appreciating it, and tending to it)
can keep us grounded—daily and throughout the rest of our lives.
Nature invites us to slow down, and in doing so, become deeply connected to the world around us. By prioritizing time in nature with
our children, we can hope to instill the value of using time wisely to
cultivate joy in simple pleasures and to care for the places we live in
and the human experiences that exist alongside them. We can also
spend time outdoors in pleasurable ways and gain a greater awareness
of how we impact and are impacted by the natural world.

A reasonable progression would be to discover our sense of place,
establish ourselves within it, and gradually take more and more responsibility for it. Sampson has suggestions for children of all ages:
"Teens and younger kids can easily be empowered to identify local
problems and devote their energies toward solutions. School gardens,
reclaimed streams, recycling programs, and fish ladders are examples
of service-based projects with the potential to build on one's understanding of local nature and deepen connections with it."[4]

Nature is all around us. It's not just for people in suburban or rural
settings, with access to sprawling landscapes. A sense of place can be
built no matter where we find ourselves. Rich, immersive nature experiences should be open and available to all children, but it is a myth
that people who live in urban landscapes cannot study nature or find
it without traveling far from their homes.

Growing up in New York City, I vividly remember that I spent
most of my summers outdoors. We were allowed to play on the block,
hide in the "woods" behind our house (which was really a small plot
of land with trees), and venture to nearby blocks around the neighborhood when riding our bikes, skateboarding, or roller-skating. We
climbed one of two trees in our tiny yard and swung from its branches.
We ran through the water of opened fire hydrants while hunting for
ladybugs. We did cartwheels through sprinklers that served us way
better than the grass they were meant to water, feeling salamanders

scurrying away beneath our feet. We never wanted to go inside. But when the streetlights turned on, we caught our last fireflies, knowing that our fun was over, and my mother would start beckoning us in for showers and food.

Where we live now, my children have renamed some of our neighborhood's natural attractions: Frogwater Pond, The Hideout, The Secret Passage, Rabbit's Meadow, Duck Lake, and Snakeskin Alley. From the sound of it, you might think that these places were grand, magical, or expansive . . . and they are, to my children. But like my own childhood experience, they are enlarged by the expanse of my children's imaginations. As adults, it is easy to complicate what is truly necessary to be absorbed by nature. Simplicity is truly a powerful means to a worthy end.

Like author Amber O'Neal Johnston, we simply want to "ensure that our children establish relationships with the land, extracting what they can for leisure, sport, enjoyment, and learning, and giving back in equal measure. We want our children to feel comfortable and welcomed in outdoor spaces. We want them to know that they belong."[5]

What Nature Teaches Us

When we visit our neighborhood nature spots, we always go expecting to see something new. That's because even the things that change slowly in the environment are still changing. Sometimes we stop to watch a turtle swim up to a school of fish, wondering what their reaction will be. Or we watch a squirrel jump from branch to branch searching for the perfect acorn. Other events require us to linger awhile. Do you know how long it takes a duck to waddle her babies to the water and teach them to swim for the first time? Or for a butterfly to emerge from its chrysalis? Let's just say, it's not quick. If you want to witness these tranquil occurrences, you must quiet your activity and *slow down*.

We do nature studies because it requires patient attention and close observation. We must take our time to truly see the beautiful things happening right around us. It develops in all of us an appreciation for the often-overlooked details and an awareness of how things grow and change.

We also spend time in nature to experience discomfort. I know—wild, right? Spending time outdoors is not always pleasant. There's a lot to contend with: adverse weather, bothersome wild animals (especially the spirited arthropod type), unfamiliar terrain, and sometimes having to push your body to work harder than it's used to. But I don't know one experience we've grown from where discomfort was not involved. Being out in nature teaches us resilience and adaptability. Nature itself shows us how things persist and survive, even as they're affected by things out of their control.

Katy Bowman, a biomechanist and author of the book *Grow Wild*, writes of the potential that nature offers from a movement perspective: "The sensory-rich outdoor environment invites us to move our bodies in complex ways while exploring with all our senses. Plus, nature settings often inspire feelings of awe, fascination, and connection with the living world around us."[6] She offers simple solutions for rendering the movement and nature deficits she sees plaguing our modern world. To know the environment around us, and to become aware of ourselves within its spaces, we need to get outside and immerse ourselves in them. We are not separate from our natural surroundings, and our overall growth, development, and learning will be enhanced by acknowledging that.

Outcomes of Time Spent Outside

Every year we do a challenge called 1000 Hours Outside. The movement is all about matching nature time with screen time. In 2021, Common Sense's media census reported that tweens were using screens an average of 5 hours and 33 minutes a day, and teens 8 hours and 39 minutes. Those numbers were up from 4 hours 44 minutes and 7 hours 22 minutes, respectively, in 2019.[7] The idea of the 1000 Hours Outside movement is that we can redirect some of those screen hours toward an important pursuit with overall health benefits. For us, whether we've completed the thousand hours each year is somewhat irrelevant. It's a guilt-free endeavor. What matters most is the intentional effort and what is gained in the process. As Ginny Yurich, the founder of the movement, writes, "The benefits of nature time have a long shelf life. If you are able to experience the relaxation response regularly, you will be much less vulnerable to the stress response in general—even when you aren't outside."[8]

In 2019, the University of Michigan published a study in *Frontiers in Psychology*[9] that showed urban dwellers experienced significantly reduced stress after spending only twenty minutes in different types of nature settings (*not* wilderness experiences already associated with healing benefits like camping or deep woods hiking). Similarly, a 2012 study showed that "four days of immersion in nature, and the corresponding disconnection from multi-media and technology, increases performance on a creativity, problem-solving task by a full 50% in a group of naive hikers . . . there is a cognitive advantage to be realized if we spend time immersed in a natural setting."[10]

I don't think anyone would necessarily be shocked by the results of these studies. Many people understand and desire the benefits of being in nature, regardless of the exact type of natural surroundings. I think what most adults struggle with is making time and space in their lives for a regular rhythm of getting outside or making it as important as other everyday demands. As a result, a generation of children is paying the cost of being distanced from nature, possibly more attached to screens than green spaces.

In the book *Last Child in the Woods: Saving Our Children from Nature-Deficit Disorder*, Richard Louv gives many heartbreaking examples of how overscheduling and lack of balance can affect our children's lives: teens who are depressed and unable to cope with mounting performance-oriented expectations, elementary schoolers who are anxiety-ridden about college, and children who long for a childhood. He notes that "instilling self-discipline is an essential value in parenting, but so is the nurturing of creativity and wonder. With greater knowledge about the measurable value of exposing children to nature, parents may have an easier time finding that balance."[11] And that's just it. The balance is what we're after. A slow approach sees time not as a commodity to be traded for doing the most, but as a generous gift toward a child's growth and maturity. Connecting with nature is an effort to maintain a healthy relationship with time and balance our children's holistic needs. By making time for it, we can reap its many rewards.

Firsthand Science

Charlotte Mason, a British educator known for her incorporation of nature studies into learning, knew all about the advantages of children honing their scientific knowledge by noticing and investigating the natural world. "Consider, too," she wrote, "what an unequalled mental training the child-naturalist is getting for any study or calling under the sun—the powers of attention, of discrimination, of patient pursuit, growing with his growth, what will they not fit him for?"[12]

The thing is, we cannot expect our children to care about or pay attention to nature if we don't do it ourselves. It's an endeavor we can pursue together, learning from each other along the way. You don't have to anticipate or know about everything you might see out on a nature walk. It might not even be the right time to rattle off your encyclopedic knowledge about slugs, birds, or whatever else was the topic of your preparatory research. When my children ask me questions, I answer if I can, but oftentimes, they know more than I do, and I'm the one asking questions. All our questions provide fertile ground for researching further at home.

When we began nature journaling, my children looked to me for guidance, but we were often experimenting with what and how to record side by side, with one another. Before I was a mother, when I was taking New York City schoolchildren to Randall's Island for nature studies, someone gifted me the books *A Trail Through Leaves* by

Hannah Hinchman and *Keeping a Nature Journal* by Clare Leslie and Charles Roth. They became invaluable to me as I began the journaling practice again, this time with my children.

Especially by the time children are older, nature studies usually get traded for more traditional science subjects, which might inadvertently overemphasize the importance of those conventional courses. That's not to say there's anything wrong with formal science study, only that doing it to the exclusion of connection to nature is limiting. Without the pressure to frantically power through curriculum, we can create space for areas of learning like nature education that are integral for well-being, awareness, centeredness, and nurturing of the mind and body. Not to mention that, in our family, spending time in nature has led to many in-depth studies (biomes, weather patterns, the water cycle, biodiversity, the moon, animal migration, rock formation, etc.) that touch a variety of traditional science fields (ecology, astronomy, biology, chemistry, botany, entomology, geology, meteorology, and more).

So many science topics typically explored with children through curriculum can be brought outside for direct experience. Food sources and climate are things you could read about in a book, but why not head outdoors and observe them up close? That is exactly why my teenage daughter would love to join an expedition with Earthwatch, an organization that connects people with scientists to help them do environmental research in the field. As Michael Caduto and Joseph Bruchac, who help educators lead hands-on environmental activities through the framework of Native American stories, write:

> Field trips are a chance to study the environment firsthand. You can visit plants and animals in their homes, learn wilderness survival skills on an extended camping trip or take a trip to a botanical garden and experience plants that come from distant lands. There is adventure in the unknown, and even familiar places look different when visited in the spirit of discovery.[13]

Growing Hope and Staying Connected

Jamila Norman, an urban farmer who helps families transform their yards into functional spaces where they too can grow food, says in a radio interview, "You can't rush nature, you got to work with it, and you have to be patient to receive the fruits of your labor as well in the garden. . . . You definitely have to have . . . a belief in the future, and that what you put in the ground now will bear fruit when you're expecting it."[14] Michael Ableman, another farmer and educator, writes of his personal experiences, "Every time I plant a seed and see it emerge, it slows me down and allows me to experience one of the great mysteries of life, and each time I cannot help but be renewed."[15] Both Norman and Ableman understand how working with nature changes their pace and calls for them to be present. I love how their work generates optimism in the land's productive ability and even in the human bonds that it builds.

Ableman also writes about how being connected with the land provides another "kind of nourishment" that is "based on relationships—local, biological, interpersonal, ecological. . . . It seems to me that real education should be based on some of those same relationships, that what we have really lost in both our food system and our education system is context, a sense of how things relate to each other."[16]

These quotes are from Ableman's book *Ecological Literacy*. The premise of ecological literacy is that by looking to ecosystems for models of sustainable communities, we can educate children about "how nature sustains the web of life."[17] If we can find ourselves entrenched in that web, "over time the experience of ecology in nature gives us a sense of place."[18] This sense of place is essential if we hope to stay grounded within the breadth of all that we can learn from the environment. Respect for the natural world is built through participation—multisensory experiences of what makes it alive and an understanding of how we are connected to it.

It wasn't until my children and I visited a couple of local community farms ourselves that we truly understood this kind of connection to our surrounding community. We saw how hard people, including volunteers, worked to care for the land. We joined them in their efforts, getting our hands dirty too. They used their best farming practices and the fruits of their labor to feed other members of the community in need. We were lending a hand to an entire system of interconnected people who were enriched by the natural systems adjacent to them. It was a valuable way for us to experience how we might nurture nature and reap a harvest.

Environmental education advocate Pamela Michael writes, "We believe that children who come to understand and to love their home places will grow into engaged, effective citizens committed to preserving those places."[19] This awareness and appreciation for what is nearby can then gradually extend out to environments that are farther away. Starting at home builds a good foundation for engagement with the wider world and contribution to the lives of others everywhere.

Environmental writer Peter Berg encouraged students to build their local knowledge by making a map of their own "bioregion." First, you make a mark representing where you live on a blank piece of paper. Then, you determine where north is and mark it on the map as well. Next, draw the nearest body of water to where you live, marking off the "watershed" (the land that surrounds the water, usually high ground, even as small as a low hill). Also mark the soil type that you see in the region (black, clay, sandy, rocky, etc.) and the native plants and animals that live there. Lastly, try to capture aspects of human relationship with the bioregion (the worst and the best).[20] When I did this with my children, they identified that overfishing in the lake near our home was upsetting the balance of wildlife (as evidenced by the growing population of aquatic midges). They also noted the strategic placement of rocks around the lake to prevent soil erosion.

That is just one idea for getting familiar with your nearby environment. If you stay observant and visit your local green spaces often, you might be surprised by how quickly the attachment grows and your sense of place is expanded. Maintaining hope about what we can learn from the experience—and from those around us who are also connected to the same place—contributes to the whole family's growth and overall wellness.

Let's not allow nature to be something that we simply see from our windows without any significant personal involvement or contact. There are various levels of participation that make space for everyone to connect. The relationship we have with nature can influence our connection to the world at large. Living an unhurried life leaves room for embracing a relationship with the natural world and stewardship of the natural systems that sustain all our lives.

I'll leave you with this encouraging invitation from Robin Wall Kimmerer's *Braiding Sweetgrass*, adapted for young adults by Monique Gray Smith:

> I invite you to remember another way of being in the world, in kinship. . . . To remember what may have been buried by the noise of the world and by the commodification of nature. A remembering of knowing you can be good medicine for the land. And I hope, a remembering of or an understanding of your gifts (something that is unique to you) and how to share them to contribute to the well-being of the world.[21]

Accepting the Invitation

Getting outside into green spaces with expectancy about the positive ways it will affect you—and even about the ways you could possibly contribute—is an active first step. Whether you're welcoming a new practice or trying to be more intentional about the degree to which you participate, there are many ways to spend time outdoors or to bring nature indoors. Doing it matters way more than doing it perfectly.

Ideas for Slowing Down in Nature

Here are a few activities and techniques my children and I have used to slow down and learn in nature. Feel free to borrow them and adapt them to your own family's needs.

NATURE WALKS

The great thing about nature walks is that you can do them just about anywhere. Just go out for a stroll on an urban street or trail or in a meadow, field, or park—it doesn't matter as long as you notice nature along the way. Sometimes it helps to have a simple focus or something you're on the lookout for (oak trees, butterflies, moss, etc.). You can use local field guides for help here. Resources like *Exploring Nature with Children* by Raising Little Shoots can give you some guidance on themes for nature walks.

HIKING

I love hiking with my family (and exploring with friends is also fun!). Join or start an adventure group to hike and investigate new trails with others, especially if you're nervous about hiking alone. Local parks and wilderness areas are great places to start.

OUTDOOR ADVENTURES

There are many activities you can do that will get you outdoors incorporating nature. Greta Eskridge's books *Adventuring Together* and *100 Days of Adventure* are full of tips for outdoor adventures, nature activities, creative projects, and field trips. Nichole Holze of the blog *Luckey Wanderers* (@coleyraeh on Instagram) also has great tips for adventuring safely alone with children.

NATURE STUDIES

There is a plethora of nature study curricula and materials out there for all ages, much of which has been created by homeschool families and small shops. I know many families who use Anna Comstock's *Handbook of Nature-Study for Teachers and Parents*. A good field guide and a willingness to research when interests arise are invaluable. We also use tools for making and recording observations such as a magnifying glass, a digital microscope, binoculars, a camera, journals, etc.

GARDENING

A garden can be a great way to encounter nature right at home. Backyard gardens, container gardens, and windowsill herb gardens are all options. You might also consider visiting or supporting a community garden or local farm.

HOUSEPLANTS AND FLOWERS

Bring the outdoors inside with houseplants. When one of my children asked me for a potted plant for his bedroom, he learned a great deal about how to care for it. It also led him to explore more about plant life in general. My children also enjoy planting flower seeds outside, cutting fresh flowers when they grow, bringing them in to adorn the table, and pressing and drying them for use with other projects.

FORAGING

Look for knowledgeable sources and guides before venturing out on your own to forage for wild edible plants. Also, be sure to research the ethics around wild foraging first. Don't assume that this isn't an option if you live in an urban area; when I lived in New York City, I foraged with "Wildman" Steve Brill in Central Park. Alexis Nikole Nelson (@blackforager on Instagram) creates foraging content that is both inspirational and educational.

BIRD-WATCHING

You can attract birds with feeders to see them a bit more closely, but you can also spot them pretty much everywhere you go outdoors.

Watching smaller birds often requires patience and stillness to spot them in their habitats. The Cornell Lab of Ornithology and the National Audubon Society (for North American birds) are great places to search for information about different bird species.

BODIES OF WATER

Finding local water sources—beaches, lakes, rivers, creeks, and so on—creates many opportunities for nature exploration. Large or small, they're a treasury of plant and animal life, and there are many things to notice about the water itself and the environment surrounding it. Various forms of precipitation can also provide experience with nature.

NATURE CENTERS

Nature centers and environmental centers are usually storehouses of information about nature in your community. Using these local resources, you might also find information about things like wild habitat restoration, urban environmentalism, or recycling education.

NATURE BOOKS

Books for nature-related topics exist in a variety of genres (nonfiction, fiction, poetry, etc.). Our local library is one of the first places we check when we're researching a new topic. You can also find book lists for nature studies from multiple sources online that will be sure to lead you to some great finds.

SOCIAL ACTIVITIES OUTSIDE

Simply take the social gatherings that occur in your life (get-togethers, meetings, celebrations) and host them in an outdoor space. The links we form with nature do not always have to be educative in nature. Sometimes they're for leisure or enjoyment.

CHAPTER 11

Connection to Others

Sharpening the Impulse to Care

Education is for improving the lives of others and for leaving your community and world better than you found it.

–MARIAN WRIGHT EDELMAN, *THE MEASURE OF OUR SUCCESS*

How should education prepare children for the future in this rapidly changing world?

The word "education" encompasses a range of processes, systems, actions, and ideas that are constantly evolving. Naturally, education is responsive to the shifts occurring in the life of a society. Throughout history, we can see how the shaping and implementation of educational ideals and goals, each with its own set of priorities and practices, became the impetus for new theories, movements, and reforms. Our aims for education are broad and complex, but as parents, we all still hope to create "lifelong learners" of our children. We want our children to be actively invested and self-motivated in their pursuit of knowledge and to have an ongoing relationship with how that knowledge is constructed, acquired, and applied.

Author and psychologist Madeline Levine phrases it like this:

The game plan for raising our kids must involve not only teaching academic curricula but also helping students develop resilience and a real appetite for lifelong learning and the challenges they are certain to encounter. Perhaps most crucially, they'll need a reliable moral compass to navigate the increasingly complex ethical challenges posed by AI and technology.[1]

Lifelong learning is not just something you do after a formal education. It's developing in a way that serves you over and over for the rest of your life, whether you're eight or eighty-eight. It's having ideas, engaging with the world around you, developing skills, adapting to change, and making your own valuable contributions. It's trying, failing, celebrating, and overcoming, connecting to the emotions of whatever the experiences bring, growing, and repeating. It's also exercising and strengthening your ability to make sound choices that are grounded by personal ethics and values.

So how does one encourage the blossoming of a lifelong learner? How can parents give their children a fighting chance of being able to navigate an uncertain future? It might help to consider the point of what we're doing in the first place.

What Is the Main Objective?

In chapter 3, I talked about the role of becoming in our greater plan for education. We slow down in order to become resilient, thoughtful, innovative learners who are committed to growth and are in it for the long haul. We don't do this just for ourselves; we're meant to make a mark in the world, no matter how large or how small.

Educator and author Vito Perrone wrote (in a chapter fittingly titled "Toward Large Purposes"):

We often speak about children and young people in our society as "the future." What do we imply by such a belief?

Preservation, or change? Ensuring that children and young people can live in the world as it is, or ensuring the skills, knowledge, and dispositions that will enable them to *change* the world, to construct on their terms new possibilities? How we think about that will say a lot about what we do in our schools, the ideas we explore, the questions we raise, the books we read, the experiences we provide.[2]

Throughout the chapter, he outlines "large hopes" for education that he believes should serve as guiding principles for how learning environments are designed. How can our children be expected to affect the lives of others in creative ways if they don't see their education as a vehicle to help them accomplish it? Or if they don't have opportunities to apply what they're learning out in the world? Like Perrone, I wonder if we're giving our children adequate tools to become integral pieces of community life. Are we helping them to comprehend how our communities are ever-changing and how they might contribute?

I don't believe that the answer is to simply make more time for less technical subjects like history, politics, or sociology on the assumption that this will engender civic-mindedness and cause our children to care for the common good. Instead, it's about having the self-awareness to find your place and figure out how you can serve others, in any subject area.

In a documentary about her life, Toni Morrison asked herself the question, "What can I do where I am?" In her book *Raising Critical Thinkers*, Julie Bogart uses Morrison's question to reflect on the whole point of education:

In the context of formal education, I hear that question this way: How can I, the person I am, in the place I am, use the tools, research, and insights of my field for the betterment of humankind—here, now? In the context of kidlets, I hear it this way: "How on Earth does this subject relate to who my child is and can be for themselves and others?" That's a powerful why for schooling, don't you agree? Let me get big and dramatic. In my opinion, we learn so that we can participate in the transformation of the world, even if that contribution means using a chemistry degree to improve the quality of shampoo. All of our contributions add up to better living (or at least, shouldn't they?).[3]

Critical thinking and reflection will ultimately lead us to consider what greater purpose our education will serve and how we can play a part in what Bogart calls "the centuries-old great conversation in our field of study, using our voices to expand the symphony of ideas, for the flourishing of all people . . . everywhere."[4]

A love for learning is not rushed. It is built through care. Caring enough about a subject to explore it, question it, understand it, and critique it. Caring about how our ideas connect to others and to the world around us. It's taking time to find those connections, test them, and think deeply about their implications. We can't just want that for our children and not for ourselves. They need to see us engaged in the "great conversation," and we need to connect with them in ways that help them to be engaged with us.

Our children also need to be firsthand witnesses to how we demonstrate our values, as they will be greatly impacted by how we implicitly and explicitly care for others or use our ideas for the good of others. The same resilience, curiosity, and creativity they need now and in the future is what we'll need too, especially as we continue to lead our families. The future is in all of our hands. As Deborah Meier writes, "If we want children to be caring and compassionate, then we must provide a place for growing up in which caring is feasible."[5]

The principles and methods I've described throughout this book are ways of pursuing knowledge that is attached to something the learner values or cares about deeply. When our children are personally invested in their work, it can spur them to formulate opinions and think and act responsibly about a host of things. Helping them to connect their work to a greater purpose can be an empowering way of guiding them toward participation in the communities around them.

No matter what philosophy or method of education we subscribe to, it should be infused with ethical reflection. No field of study is devoid of ethical questions. Commensurate with their age and understanding, we can help our children to examine the values that underpin all ideas. They are evident in the choices, actions, research, practices, and communication that all academic disciplines call into question. We can also help our children to notice the complexities when they exist, make their own decisions, and consider in retrospect how their values impacted their actions.

Values are certainly a key piece of a meaningful education. However, a value is not just something we possess. To be others-aware, we must realize that value is also meant to be poured out. We offer it to the world by the ways we choose to contribute. Our education and our lives of learning should be a factor in how we attempt to live more generously.

Consumption vs. Contribution

We all have a desire to feel significant. We want to know that our lives have value, that we're making an impact, that our existence is meaningful. As a result, we look for a source of that significance. We look for the one thing we can turn to and say, "Yes, *this* is what makes me so valuable." My husband, Jordan, calls this the "Source Principle."[6]

There are two ways we can fulfill this need for significance in our lives: consumption and contribution. Consumption means that we're taking from people or things in a way that makes us feel important. Contribution means that we're giving to people or things in a way that demonstrates our value and our worth.

Giving value goes beyond needing others to make us feel important or to determine the extent of our usefulness. When we contribute to the lives of others in meaningful ways, guided by the principles that govern how we live, we show up at 100 percent, ready to intentionally serve. We can teach our children that if they go through life expecting more from others than what others can expect from them, they're consuming more than they're contributing. All this education should help them to discover how much value they actually have to give.

The greatest level of contribution is found in service—in meeting the needs of others. If we want to serve humanity, if we want our children to serve humanity, then we must learn to look for the needs. In a general sense, most of us are used to meeting the needs of others (like our loved ones) out of a sense of duty or requirement. But recognizing a need includes actively looking for ways to contribute to our families and our communities at large that go beyond obligation. It also involves seeking out connections between the things we learn, study, and experience and how they can be enacted in age-appropriate, service-oriented ways. It doesn't exclude partnerships with others to address issues and problems. We can add value through collaborative efforts. The possibilities are endless. We need only to be open to them.

Since our concern is most easily directed to those inside our familiar circles, our challenge is to help our children extend themselves to others outside of that circle. Ideally, our children would get to witness the family prioritizing interest in things happening beyond the borders of home and being regularly engaged with communities, even if it's outside their comfort zone. Our children should see that others' needs matter just as much as the needs of the family.

Prioritizing caring also helps our children to consistently honor the commitments they make as part of their service, even the ones that come at the expense of their own comfort. When my brother and I were younger, he had a paper route. Every single day of the week, he delivered newspapers to subscribers along a fixed route, which included houses, businesses, and a nursing home. At some point, when it became a lot for him to manage, he asked me to help him. I didn't love it. Some of the customers were downright mean, and it exasperated me that my brother put up with them. Others were generous and kind and even gave us special gifts around the holidays.

Once, after a particularly exhausting day when a nursing home resident spat at us, I came home and announced to my mother that I was quitting. I'll never forget how she sat there with the both of us and encouraged us to honor our commitments, while at the same time helping us to problem-solve about the issues we were having with particular customers. By the end, we felt empowered to speak up for ourselves. I understood that quitting would only leave my brother in a more tenuous position. We were stronger together. My service was in support of my own family member, and after all these years, I'm still grateful for the valuable lesson my mother taught us that day.

Growing the Head and the Heart

In a 1947 article called "The Purpose of Education," written for Morehouse College's student newspaper, Martin Luther King Jr. penned these words: "Education must enable one to sift and weigh evidence, to discern the true from the false, the real from the unreal, and the facts from the fiction. The function of education, therefore, is to teach one to think intensively and to think critically. But education which stops with efficiency may prove the greatest menace to society. The most dangerous criminal may be the man gifted with reason, but with no morals." King urged, "We must remember that intelligence is not enough. Intelligence plus character—that is the goal of true education."[7]

Growing and learning about who we are, what our interests and passions are, how we can contribute to the world, and how we can become better humans might seem lofty, but truly that is what education is about. Of paramount importance are our opportunities to help our children think intellectually *and* make sound moral judgments that demonstrate respect for themselves and concern for others. All the content knowledge we focus on acquiring (like in reading, writing, and math) serves a greater purpose than solely being the barometer of academic success. These subjects are the tools we need to access and explore bigger ideas. What good are all those scholastic skills if we can't use them to express original thoughts, build a bridge, structure a business, or cook a meal? If they can't give access to a rich world where our contribution matters?

One day, while I was grocery shopping with my son, he was talking to me about cars. A store employee overheard him and couldn't help asking my son some questions. Before long they were both excitedly discussing methods for powering a vehicle. They weighed the pros and cons of various types of fuel, both traditional and alternative. When we walked away, my son turned to me and said, "I'm starting to think that math and science could really change the world. I think I want to be a part of that. There are so many powerful tools that can do a lot of good, but at the same time, they can be used for destruction. I want to help evolve things but also be responsible." I was so grateful for this unexpected conversation that helped him to see the bigger picture.

We can use these academic avenues as the training ground for organizing the information and analyzing the data we are barraged with daily, to improve the lives of others while carrying a sense of hope and optimism about it all. We add to this world from the moment we're born into it. Slow schooling exists to help our children to figure out how. The influence we have and the value that we can give are not siloed in adulthood. We are all responsible for one another, and without empathy and compassion, the academics mean very little. We are using the power of slow to help to develop our children as engaged participants, stewards, and contributors to the world they live in. We are meant to do much more than consume.

Conclusion

There is more to life than increasing its speed.

—MAHATMA GANDHI

In 2020, I trained for a 5K race I never actually ran. Well, really, there was no *official* race. I simply decided that I wanted to run a 5K in a certain amount of time, so I got my body up to speed (no pun intended). Although I put myself through multiple strength and cardio drills, much of the work was more mental than physical. Many days, I told myself I couldn't do it before I even tried. But by the time I finally conquered my goal, I no longer believed that it was difficult.

Have you ever reacted to something someone else is doing by saying, "Oh, I could never do that"? Have you ever told someone about something you do, and they had the same reaction toward you? Our ideas about the difficulty of other ways of doing things are usually skewed by our commitment (or lack thereof) to what we're familiar with. Things end up feeling easier when we intentionally commit to doing them or put them into practice. Something can feel less difficult simply because it's familiar, we've made it a routine, or we've created space for it in our minds and hearts. Meanwhile, we know good and well that parts of what we're calling easy are actually difficult or demanding.

Nothing is ever entirely easy. Nothing is without risk or consequences. We simply commit to things that matter to us. So don't assume that you could "never" do something. Just decide what matters. If there's any part of your life about which you feel the need to slow down, bring balance, and be way more intentional, I hope you find the courage to do it.

Being responsible for your child's education, to whatever degree you have chosen, certainly has its challenges. But it is doable. It can also be enjoyable and very rewarding. I hope you walk away from this book not with a blueprint for exactly how slow schooling "should" be done but with tools to help you to imagine possibilities for your own family. Your family is unique, and the pace that you set for it is something only you can determine.

Remember that in the end, slow is an effort to be more balanced. Balance helps us to make better choices for ourselves and for our families that are both sensible *and* meaningful. We're more likely to find joy when we're living a meaningful life, or when our lives are full of experiences that hold intrinsic value.

Slow schooling is a beautiful blend of resisting the urge to hurry and accelerating when it makes sense to do so. Knowing your child and knowing when that means more than how they're measured by a system. Doing what's important and making the simple important enough. Being present and being willing to prune what gets your attention. Going with the flow and going against the grain. Asking questions and being okay with not having all the answers.

We can take time and give time and gain so much in the process. Here's to the joy of slow.

Acknowledgments

No one writes a book alone. When you pour yourself out upon the pages within, inevitably they will bear the imprints of a life lived with others. I have so much gratitude for the people who have impacted my story and who have helped me to get here.

My dear husband, Jordan, this book would not have happened without you! I love bouncing around ideas with you and using them to dream and decide how we will parent and live. Thank you for lending me your best ones and letting me shape them for my personal work. Thank you for always seeing things in me that I don't realize are there and for protecting the areas where I feel vulnerable. You daily encourage me to look higher, go deeper, and be better. I love you so very much. You are not only my idea person but also my prayer partner, support, safe place, comedic relief, and best friend.

Mya, Caden, Ethan, and Myles, you four made me a mother and awakened things in me that have changed me forever. Thank you for your patience and encouragement while I wrote this book. Every time I asked you to let me finish a thought, help with making a meal, suggest a synonym for a word—all of it. I am so grateful for your willingness to support me. I've joked that people would never believe the circumstances under which this book was written. Sometimes, I was writing in the middle of pure chaos! But that doesn't change the fact that you four are amazing and that I love you! Not to mention, I would have nothing to put in the pages of this book if it wasn't for you. Each one of you is a bright individual, full of imagination and strength. You have so much to offer this world, and I never want you to forget that. I love the life we have created together!

Mom and Dad, the way that you both support me and the things I do moves me to tears. Thank you for always believing in me and for encouraging me to use my gifts. You nurtured creativity and wonder in me from the start, and I know how proud of me you are for this book. I daily feel your prayers and experience your care. I love you both so much. I think Eric would have loved this too. I wish he was here to read it and celebrate with us.

Mom Martino, Melissa, Jay, Leslie, Adam, and all the Martino children, thank you for loving me. Period. We've been bonded for the past thirty-some-odd years, and my life is infinitely better because of it. Mom, you've been pouring love, wisdom, and encouragement into me for a long time, and you will forever have a piece of my heart. I still look back at my younger, teenage self, and I know I wouldn't be the woman I am today without you.

My agent, Anna Knutson Geller, you believed in this book from the very start. You also understood my message in a way that encouraged me deeply. I cried through those initial iterations of what this book would become, but every step helped to develop me as a writer and refine my ideas. This was all due to your rich insight and thoughtful advice. I am forever grateful.

My editor, Lauren O'Neal, and the entire team at TarcherPerigee, thank you for helping to breathe life into this book. Your meaningful feedback and close attention meant the world to me. Lauren, your clear communication helped me through this entire process, and from our first conversation, you put me at ease and demonstrated that I was in good hands.

Joanna Ng, I will never forget the connection I felt with you early on. Thank you for hearing my voice and understanding my message. You gently directed my writing and helped me to see how I could grow.

Ainsley Arment, you, my dear friend, are the original "slow

school" advocate, and there are not enough words to describe the value and wisdom you add to the homeschool space. Thank you for sharing my voice with the Wild + Free community and for writing the beautiful foreword for this book. Your encouragement and confidence in me mean so much, and it is a joy to be connected to you.

Julie Bogart, we share the same publisher, and I know that my book would never have been given a second look if it hadn't been for the one you published in 2019. You laid the groundwork for a force of women ready to spread a message of love, wonder, and curiosity in learning, and for that, I thank you. Because of you, *I* am a Brave Learner and a Brave Writer.

Sally Clarkson, thank you for your thoughtful attention and concern for me as a writer, and as a person. I can still remember you brainstorming with me about book ideas the first time we met. You have a gift for "narrating forward" the good qualities you see in others, and when you first did that for me, it left me in tears and feeling very seen. You are a mother of mothers. Thank you for folding me into your love and wisdom.

My cousins, Jeff, Tiffany, Dimitri, and Amanda, thank you for taking the kids on epic adventures so that I could write. It is so meaningful to me how you love hard by finding practical ways to help. If there is anyone who has valued and supported my voice before I was ever even on Instagram, it's all of you. You've been championing me from way back when. Even though I get incredibly embarrassed when you brag about me in public, the truth is, it makes me feel honored. Jeff and Dimitri, I'm the "big sister" you never wanted (ha!), but you are the "little brothers" I am so lucky to have.

Jason, Leslie, and Grace Rewis (soon to be Clark), there are no words for what you all mean to my family. Thank you for being you. Thank you for being excited with me. Thank you for cheering me on. Thank you for giving me ideas. Thank you for asking how I'm doing. Thank you for feeding me. Thank you for doing all that you do. I love you all.

To the entire McMullen family, thank you for your love, and Jason, for your sound advice early on in this process. I will always remember Puerto Rico with you all as a much-needed rest and celebration of my manuscript being complete. All of the laughter was so good for the soul.

Deborah Healy, my ride-or-die, my partner in crime, the OG! You've been with me through it all, and I'm so glad God saw fit to unite us all those years ago. Thank you for being you and for allowing me to be me. Technically, you wrote this book too because we will forever be Les-Deb!

Serena Johnson, my sister, what can I say? Thank you for doing life with me and for walking with me through all of my joys, triumphs, missteps, heartaches, and everything in between. You teach me so much about grace, intentionality, and genuine selflessness. You are the real deal. Celebrating this book with you feels amazing because you were with me through the journey, and we both know how much it's a testimony of God's kindness and faithfulness. I love you.

Amber O'Neal Johnston, my sweet friend, where would I be without you? I sometimes feel terrible that we talk and devise plans for me, based on all the losses and wins that you had to personally experience. But it highlights a simple fact: You're a way-paver and a trailblazer. Thank you for treading this path ahead of me, holding my hand, and encouraging me the whole way through. I knew we'd be close friends from the moment we met. Can't wait for our next tea date or late-night Thai food gab fest. I am forever in your corner.

Greta Eskridge, if Voxer only knew the role it played in the writing of this book! We have shared advice and encouragement. We have traded family stories and writing processes. Sharing that with an accomplished author, but more importantly, a friend, was invaluable. Thank you for being a listening ear and always willing to take me along (figuratively, of course) on your life adventures.

Elsie Ludicello, you are such a gift. I'm not sure I've ever met anyone who encourages me in the way that you do. Thank you for your constant sound counsel and for urging me to do things even when I'm nervous or lack confidence. You are a good friend, and you inspire me greatly.

Torrie Oglesby, something has to be said for women who lift up other women and who use their intuition and sensitivity to bolster others. That's what you do for me, and I just need to say thank you. I'm so glad I sent you that crazy IG message four years ago!

A big shout-out to my Book Club group, PE moms, and local Wild + Free group. I'm not sure you realize how much I enjoy the time we spend together. We casually talk about so many big ideas, and all the while, we are challenging and supporting one another. Thank you for helping me to grow. Thank you for being my cheerleaders as I have shared my hopes and goals with you. Everyone needs friends like you!

To my COL church family back in New York (you know who you are), I love you. Thank you for carrying me with your prayers.

To my DFC church family, thank you for your words of encouragement, support, prayers, and love. The way you uphold my family is incredibly special and wonderful.

All of my dear friends whom I did not mention by name, you are not forgotten. You have pushed me through this process by being a light and encouragement like only a true friend could. I will never take that for granted. Thank you for laughing with me, distracting me, checking in on me, scolding me, supporting me, and loving me.

To every child, parent, teacher, colleague, and educator who has helped to shape my ideas about education, thank you. You deserve the joy of knowing that your labor is not in vain. Neither is your love. Both have marked me forever.

Lastly, I want to thank YOU, my lovely readers, for uniting with me in celebrating the joy of slow. It is an honor to continue side by side with you in the work of homeschooling and parenting. I had no idea that starting to hashtag #slowschooljoy and sharing my heart publicly and privately would connect me to so many wonderful families. Keep going! What you are doing is so important.

Notes

Chapter 1: First Things First

1. David Bensman, *Quality Education in the Inner City: The Story of the Central Park East Schools* (New Brunswick, NJ: Rutgers University, 1987), 21.

2. Harry R. Lewis to the Harvard student, "Slow Down: Getting More Out of Harvard by Doing Less," January 9, 2004, University Hall, Harvard College, Cambridge, MA, https://lewis.seas.harvard.edu/files/harrylewis/files /slowdown2004_0.pdf.

3. Lawrence Baines, "Learning from the World: Achieving More by Doing Less," *The Phi Delta Kappan* 89, no. 2 (2007): 100, http://www.jstor.org /stable/20442426.

4. Gerald W. Bracey, *A Short Guide to Standardized Testing* (Bloomington, IN: Phi Delta Kappa Educational Foundation, 2000), 45–46.

5. Alfie Kohn, "Moving beyond Facts, Skills, and Right Answers," *Alfie Kohn*, 1999, https://www.alfiekohn.org/article/moving-beyond-facts-skills-right -answers.

6. Ainsley Arment, *The Call of the Wild and Free: Reclaiming Wonder in Your Child's Education* (San Francisco: HarperOne, 2019), 157.

7. Julie Bogart, "Rigor vs. Relaxed Alertness: The Sweet Spot," September 2020, in *Brave Writer*, podcast, audio, 15:54, https://blog.bravewriter.com /2020/09/02/podcast-rigor-vs-relaxed-alertness.

8. Frank Smith, *The Book of Learning and Forgetting* (New York: Teachers College Press, 1998), 13.

9. "Researcher Gloria Ladson-Billings on Culturally Relevant Teaching, the Role of Teachers," interview by The 74, Wisconsin Center for Education Research, December 30, 2019, https://www.wcer.wisc.edu/news/detail/researcher-gloria-ladson-billings-on-culturally-relevant-teaching-the-role.

10. John Taylor Gatto, *Dumbing Us Down: The Hidden Curriculum of Compulsory Schooling*, 2nd ed. (Gabriola Island, British Colombia: New Society Publishers, 2002), 29.

11. Gatto, *Dumbing Us Down*, xxxvi.

12. Marianne Sunderland, "A Surprising Benefit of Homeschooling," *Homeschooling with Dyslexia*, January 8, 2022, https://homeschoolingwithdyslexia.com/benefit-of-homeschooling.

13. Lori McWilliam Pickert, *Project-Based Homeschooling: Mentoring Self-Directed Learners* (Scotts Valley, CA: CreateSpace Independent Publishing Platform, 2012), 10.

14. Melissa Wiley, "What Is Tidal Homeschooling," *Here in the Bonny Glen*, updated January 2023, https://melissawiley.com/tidal-homeschooling.

15. Grace Llewellyn, *The Teenage Liberation Handbook: How to Quit School and Get a Real Life and Education*, 3rd ed. (Eugene, OR: Lowry House, 2021), 135.

Chapter 2: Building the Foundation

1. Billy Collins, "On Slowing Down" (speech, Wallingford, CT, Summer 2003), National Association of Independent Schools, https://www.nais.org/magazine/independent-school/summer-2003/on-slowing-down/.

2. Alfred North Whitehead, *The Aims of Education and Other Essays*, reissue ed. (New York: Free Press, 1967), 29.

3. Mike Rose, *The Mind at Work: Valuing the Intelligence of the American Worker* (New York: Penguin Books, 2004), 99.

4. David Elkind, *The Power of Play: Learning What Comes Naturally* (Boston: Da Capo Press, 2007), 209–10.

5. "The Four Educative Drives," The Alliance for Self-Directed Education, accessed October 2022, https://www.self-directed.org/sde/drives.

6. Blake Boles, *Why Are You Still Sending Your Kids to School?: The Case for Helping Them Leave, Chart Their Own Paths, and Prepare for Adulthood at Their Own Pace* (Loon Lake, CA: Tells Peak Press, 2020), 113.

7. Boles, *Why Are You Still Sending Your Kids to School?*, 121.

8. Susan Linn, *The Case for Make Believe: Saving Play in a Commercialized World* (New York: The New Press, 2009), 197.

9. Linn, *The Case for Make Believe*, 197.

10. Linn, *The Case for Make Believe*, 200.

Chapter 3: Core Values

1. Marc Prensky, "The Goal of Education Is Becoming," *Education Week*, May 5, 2014, https://www.edweek.org/leadership/opinion-the-goal-of -education-is-becoming/2014/05.

2. Erin Loechner, *Chasing Slow: Courage to Journey Off the Beaten Path* (Grand Rapids, MI: Zondervan, 2016), 263.

3. Loechner, *Chasing Slow*, 264.

4. Julie Bogart, "Practicing Psychological Flexibility and ACT with Dr. Diana Hill," May 2021, in *Brave Writer*, podcast, audio, 56:15, https://blog .bravewriter.com/2021/05/05/podcast-practicing-psychological-flexibility -dr-diana-hill.

5. Madeline Levine, *Teach Your Children Well: Parenting for Authentic Success* (New York: Harper, 2012), 251–52.

6. Levine, *Teach Your Children Well*, 255.

7. Jordan Martino, "Expectation," webinar at Deeper Fellowship Church, January 16, 2023.

8. Alfred North Whitehead, *The Aims of Education and Other Essays*, reissue ed. (New York: Free Press, 1967), 29.

Chapter 4: Home as Haven

1. Julie Lasky, "Hay House: How Designer Sheila Bridges Made Space for Herself," *The New York Times*, March 25, 2022, https://www.nytimes.com /2022/03/25/realestate/sheila-bridges-hay-house-interview.html.

2. Marie Kondo, "KonMari Is Not Minimalism," KonMari Media, accessed January 2023, https://konmari.com/konmari-is-not-minimalism.

3. Jura Koncius, "Marie Kondo's Life Is Messier Now—and She's Fine with It," *The Washington Post*, January 26, 2023, https://www.washingtonpost .com/home/2023/01/26/marie-kondo-kurashi-inner-calm.

4. "Marie Kondo Gave Up on Tidying . . . Now What? A Pro Organizer's Take," The Organized Soprano, February 2, 2023, video, 0:03:30, https://www.youtube.com/watch?v=mQona2YpIho.

5. S. D. Smith, *Ember Falls* (Beaver, WV: Story Warren Books, 2016), 164–65.

6. Maria Montessori, *Pedagogical Anthropology* (New York: Frederick A. Stokes Company, 1913), 17, quoted in Rita Kramer, *Maria Montessori: A Biography* (Boston: Da Capo Press, 1976), 98.

7. Gordon Neufeld and Gabor Maté, *Hold On to Your Kids: Why Parents Need to Matter More Than Peers* (Toronto: Vintage Canada, 2013), 184.

8. Elizabeth Enright, *The Saturdays* (New York: Dell, 1941), 104.

9. Makoto Fujimura, *Art and Faith: A Theology of Making* (New Haven, CT: Yale University Press, 2020).

10. Fujimura, *Art and Faith*, 43.

11. Fujimura, *Art and Faith*, 44–45.

12. Rich Karlgaard, *Late Bloomers: The Hidden Strengths of Learning and Succeeding at Your Own Pace* (New York: Broadway Books, 2020), 14.

13. Karlgaard, *Late Bloomers*, 15–16.

14. Charlotte M. Mason, *Parents and Children*, rev. ed. (London: Kegan Paul, Trench, Trübner, 1904), 32, 248.

15. Leah Boden, *Modern Miss Mason: Discover How Charlotte Mason's Revolutionary Ideas on Home Education Can Change How You & Your Children Learn & Grow Together* (Carol Stream, IL: Tyndale Momentum, 2022), 36.

16. Jennifer Pepito, *Mothering by the Book: The Power of Reading Aloud to Overcome Fear and Recapture Joy* (Minneapolis: Bethany House, 2022), 87.

17. Maya Angelou, *All God's Children Need Traveling Shoes* (New York: Vintage Books, 1986), 196.

18. Deborah Meier, "The Kindergarten Tradition in the High School," in *Progressive Education for the 1990s: Transforming Practice*, ed. Kathe Jervis and Carol Montag (New York: Teachers College Press, 1991), 136.

19. Meier, "The Kindergarten Tradition in the High School," 136.

20. Loris Malaguzzi, in *The Hundred Languages of Children: The Reggio Emilia Approach—Advanced Reflections*, 2nd ed., ed. Carolyn Edwards, Lella Gandini, and George Forman (Greenwich, CT: Ablex, 1998), 177.

Chapter 5: Establishing Routines

1. Margaret Mann Phillips, *Erasmus on His Times: A Shortened Version of the "Adages" of Erasmus* (Cambridge: Cambridge University Press, 1967), 3.

2. Phillips, *Erasmus on His Times*, 5.

3. Justin Whitmel Earley, *Habits of the Household: Practicing the Story of God in Everyday Family Rhythms* (Grand Rapids, MI: Zondervan, 2021), 9.

4. Greg McKeown, *Essentialism: The Disciplined Pursuit of Less* (New York: Currency, 2014), 126.

5. McKeown, *Essentialism*, 129.

6. McKeown, *Essentialism*, 189.

7. McKeown, *Essentialism*, 187.

8. McKeown, *Essentialism*, 184.

9. Julie Bogart, *The Brave Learner: Finding Everyday Magic in Homeschool, Learning, and Life* (New York: TarcherPerigee, 2019), 178.

10. Mihaly Csikszentmihalyi, *Creativity: Flow and the Psychology of Discovery and Invention* (New York: HarperPerennial, 1996), 353.

Chapter 6: Project Time

1. Kim John Payne, *Simplicity Parenting: Using the Extraordinary Power of Less to Raise Calmer, Happier, and More Secure Kids* (New York: Ballantine Books, 2010), 161.

2. John Holt, *Learning All the Time: How Small Children Begin to Read, Write, Count, and Investigate the World, without Being Taught* (Boston: Da Capo Lifelong Books, 1990), 162.

3. Lori McWilliam Pickert, *Project-Based Homeschooling: Mentoring Self-Directed Learners* (Scotts Valley, CA: CreateSpace Independent Publishing Platform, 2012), 9.

4. Isabela Granic, Adam Lobel, and Rutger C. M. E. Engels, "The Benefits of Playing Video Games," *American Psychologist* 69, no. 1 (January 2014): 66, 70, https://www.apa.org/pubs/journals/releases/amp-a0034857.pdf.

5. Lori Pickert, "The Sliver, or How to Stop Fighting about Screen Time" *Camp Creek Blog*, Project-Based Homeschooling, May 15, 2013, http://project -based-homeschooling.com/camp-creek-blog/sliver-or-how-stop-fighting -about-screen-time.

6. "How Do People Practice SDE?" The Alliance for Self-Directed Education, accessed August 2022, https://www.self-directed.org/sde/how.

7. Loris Malaguzzi, "100 Languages," trans. Lella Gandini, created by Reggio Children, Reggio Emilia Approach, accessed August 2022, https://www .reggiochildren.it/en/reggio-emilia-approach/100-linguaggi-en.

8. Leslie Martino, "Seeing Possibility in Our Children's Strengths," *Wild + Free WHISPER Bundle*, September 2021.

9. Patricia F. Carini, "A Letter to Parents and Teachers on Some Ways of Looking at and Reflecting on Children," *From Another Angle: Children's Strengths and School Standards*, ed. Margaret Himley (New York: Teachers College Press, 2000), 64.

10. Patricia F. Carini, "Building from Children's Strengths," *The Journal of Education* 168, no. 3 (1986): 20–22, http://www.jstor.org/stable /42741752.

Chapter 7: Learning at a Different Tempo

1. Tania Luna and LeeAnn Renninger, *Surprise: Embrace the Unpredictable and Engineer the Unexpected* (New York: Perigee, 2015), 35.

2. Luna and Renninger, *Surprise*, 41.

3. Manoush Zomorodi, *Bored and Brilliant: How Spacing Out Can Unlock Your Most Productive and Creative Self* (New York: St. Martin's Press, 2017), 144.

4. Zomorodi, *Bored and Brilliant*, 145.

5. Zomorodi, *Bored and Brilliant*, 146.

6. "Poetry Teatime," Brave Writer, accessed February 2023, https://bravewriter .com/program/brave-writer-lifestyle/poetry-teatimes.

7. "About," The Florida Frontiersmen, Inc., accessed February 2023, https:// www.floridafrontiersmen.org/?page_id=2.

8. Amber O'Neal Johnston, *A Place to Belong: Celebrating Diversity and Kinship in the Home and Beyond* (New York: TarcherPerigee, 2022), 17.

9. Kwame Alexander, "How to Get Kids Hooked on Books? 'Use Poetry. It Is a Surefire Way,'" interview by NPR, April 3, 2016, https://www.npr.org /2016/04/03/472859082/how-to-hook-kids-on-books-try-poetry.

10. Leslie Martino, "Woven Stories," *Wild + Free HERITAGE Bundle*, May 2021.

11. bell hooks, *Teaching Critical Thinking: Practical Wisdom* (New York: Routledge, 2010), 44.

12. hooks, *Teaching Critical Thinking*, 45.

13. hooks, *Teaching Critical Thinking*, 47.

14. Rae Jacobson, "Helping Kids with Flexible Thinking," Child Mind Institute, updated December 15, 2021, https://childmind.org/article /helping-kids-with-flexible-thinking.

15. Eleanor Duckworth, "The Virtues of Not Knowing," *The Having of Wonderful Ideas: And Other Essays on Teaching and Learning* (New York: Teachers College Press, 1987), 67.

16. Duckworth, *The Having of Wonderful Ideas*, 67.

17. Duckworth, *The Having of Wonderful Ideas*, 67.

18. Duckworth, *The Having of Wonderful Ideas*, 68.

19. "What Are the Five Common Topics of Dialectic?" Classical Conversations, updated September 26, 2022, https://classicalconversations.com/blog/five -common-topics-of-dialectic.

20. Richard W. Paul, *Critical Thinking: How to Prepare Students for a Rapidly Changing World* (Santa Rosa, CA: Foundation for Critical Thinking, 1993), 341.

21. Paul, *Critical Thinking*, 341–44.

22. Laura Grace Weldon, "Keeping Creativity Alive," March 12, 2015, https:// lauragraceweldon.com/2015/03/12/keeping-creativity-alive.

23. Keith Sawyer, "What You Do Afterwards," The Creativity Guru, December 11, 2017, https://keithsawyer.wordpress.com/2017/12/11/what-you-do -afterwards.

24. Vito Perrone, *A Letter to Teachers: Reflections on Schooling and the Art of Teaching* (San Francisco: Jossey-Bass, 1991), 9.

25. Oliver Burkeman, *Four Thousand Weeks: Time Management for Mortals* (New York: Farrar, Straus and Giroux, 2021), 165–66.

26. Susan Wise Bauer, *The Well-Educated Mind: A Guide to the Classical Education You Never Had* (New York: W. W. Norton, 2003), 26.

27. Julie Bogart, *Raising Critical Thinkers: A Parent's Guide to Growing Wise Kids in the Digital Age* (New York: TarcherPerigee, 2022), 172.

28. Julia Brodsky, *Bright, Brave, Open Minds: Engaging Young Children in Math Inquiry* (Cary, NC: Delta Stream Media, 2016), 9–10.

29. Deborah Meier, "The Kindergarten Tradition in the High School," in *Progressive Education for the 1990s: Transforming Practice*, ed. Kathe Jervis and Carol Montag (New York: Teachers College Press, 1991), 138.

30. Michael Rucker, "We Are Critically Fun Starved," January 3, 2023, in *The 1000 Hours Outside*, podcast, audio, 27:21, https://1000hoursoutside.libsyn .com/1kho-109-we-are-critically-fun-starved-michael-rucker-phd-the-fun -habit.

31. Merriam-Webster.com Dictionary, s.v. "spontaneous," accessed March 11, 2023, https://www.merriam-webster.com/dictionary/spontaneous.

32. Betty Edwards, *Drawing on the Right Side of the Brain*, 4th ed. (New York: TarcherPerigee, 2012), 248.

33. Michael Easter, *The Comfort Crisis: Embrace Discomfort to Reclaim Your Wild, Happy, Healthy Self* (New York: Rodale Books, 2021), 62.

34. Barbara Oakley, *A Mind for Numbers: How to Excel at Math and Science* (New York: TarcherPerigee, 2014), 168–82.

35. Sharon M. Draper, *Teaching from the Heart: Reflections, Encouragement, and Inspiration* (Portsmouth, NH: Heinemann, 2000), 79–81.

Chapter 8: Tools for Measuring Growth

1. John Denver, "Garden Song," accessed May 9, 2023, https://genius.com /John-denver-garden-song-lyrics.

2. Laurent Schwartz, *A Mathematician Grappling with His Century*, trans. Leila Schneps (Basel, Switzerland: Birkhäuser Verlag, 2001), 30.

3. Schwartz, *A Mathematician Grappling with His Century*, 31.

4. Howard E. Gruber, "The Time It Takes to Think," in *Building on the Strengths of Children*, ed. Vivian O. Windley, Miriam Selchen Dorn, and

Lillian Weber (New York, NY: Weekend Institute, Department of Elementary Education of the City College School of Education, 1981), 18–21.

5. Patricia F. Carini and Margaret Himley, *Jenny's Story: Taking the Long View of the Child* (New York: Teachers College Press, 2010), 52.

6. Keith Devlin, *The Math Gene: How Mathematical Thinking Evolved and Why Numbers Are Like Gossip* (New York: Basic Books, 2000), 4.

7. Devlin, *The Math Gene*, 7.

8. Luba Vangelova, "5-Year-Olds Can Learn Calculus," *The Atlantic*, March 3, 2014, https://www.theatlantic.com/education/archive/2014/03/5-year-olds -can-learn-calculus/284124.

9. Vangelova, "5-Year-Olds Can Learn Calculus."

10. Lauren B. Resnick, *Education and Learning to Think* (Washington, DC: National Academy Press, 1987), 8.

11. Margaret Himley and Patricia F. Carini, eds., *From Another Angle: Children's Strengths and School Standards* (New York: Teachers College Press, 2000), 57.

12. Himley and Carini, *From Another Angle*, 57.

13. Himley and Carini, *From Another Angle*, 58–64.

14. Patricia F. Carini, "Made by Hand (2007)," *Schools: Studies in Education* 13, no. 2 (2016): 263–72, https://www.jstor.org/stable/26562419.

Chapter 9: Connection through Relationship

1. Sally and Sarah Clarkson, *The Lifegiving Home: Creating a Place of Belonging and Becoming* (Carol Stream, IL: Tyndale Momentum, 2016), 68.

2. Kim John Payne with Lisa M. Ross, *Simplicity Parenting: Using the Extraordinary Power of Less to Raise Calmer, Happier, and More Secure Kids* (New York: Ballantine Books, 2009), 115.

3. Pam Leo, "Connection Parenting," conference presentation at Wild + Free, Franklin, TN, September 18, 2021.

4. Gordon Neufeld and Gabor Maté, *Hold On to Your Kids: Why Parents Need to Matter More Than Peers* (Toronto: Vintage Canada, 2013), 74.

5. Neufeld and Maté, *Hold On to Your Kids*, 218.

6. Neufeld and Maté, *Hold On to Your Kids*, 218–19.

7. Laura Markham, "5 Secrets for a Closer Bond with Your Child," Aha! Parenting, accessed May 19, 2023, https://www.ahaparenting.com/read/nurturing-intimacy.

8. Kim John Payne and Luis Fernando Llosa, *Emotionally Resilient Tweens and Teens: Empowering Your Kids to Navigate Bullying, Teasing, and Social Exclusion* (Boulder, CO: Shambhala Publications, 2022), 13.

9. Toni Morrison, "Does Your Face Light Up?" Oprah Winfrey Network, November 2, 2011, video, 0:00:39, https://www.youtube.com/watch?v=9Jw0Fu8nhOc.

10. Ainsley Arment, *The Wild + Free Family: Forging Your Own Path to a Life Full of Wonder, Adventure, and Connection* (New York: HarperOne, 2022), 21.

Chapter 10: Connection to the Natural World

1. Greta Eskridge, *Adventuring Together: How to Create Connections and Make Lasting Memories with Your Kids* (Nashville: Nelson Books, 2020), 75.

2. Scott D. Sampson, *How to Raise a Wild Child: The Art and Science of Falling in Love with Nature* (New York: First Mariner Books, 2016), 62.

3. Sampson, *How to Raise a Wild Child*, 63–64.

4. Sampson, *How to Raise a Wild Child*, 210.

5. Amber O'Neal Johnston, *A Place to Belong: Celebrating Diversity and Kinship in the Home and Beyond* (New York: TarcherPerigee, 2022), 174.

6. Katy Bowman, *Grow Wild: The Whole-Child, Whole-Family Nature-Rich Guide to Moving More* (Carlsborg, WA: Propriometrics Press, 2021) 20, Kindle.

7. Victoria Rideout et al., *Common Sense Census: Media Use by Tweens and Teens, 2021* (San Francisco: Common Sense, March 2022), https://www.commonsensemedia.org/sites/default/files/research/report/8-18-census-integrated-report-final-web_0.pdf.

8. Ginny Yurich, *1000 Hours Outside: Prioritize Nature, Reclaim Childhood, and Experience a Fuller Life* (Sunflower House Books, 2022), 103.

9. MaryCarol R. Hunter, Brenda W. Gillespie, and Sophie Yu-Pu Chen, "Urban Nature Experiences Reduce Stress in the Context of Daily Life Based on Salivary Biomarkers," *Frontiers in Psychology* 10 (April 2019), https://doi.org/10.3389/fpsyg.2019.00722.

10. Ruth Ann Atchley, David L. Strayer, and Paul Atchley, "Creativity in the Wild: Improving Creative Reasoning through Immersion in Natural Settings," *PLOS ONE* 7, no. 12 (December 2012): e51474, https://doi.org /10.1371/journal.pone.0051474.

11. Richard Louv, *Last Child in the Woods: Saving Our Children from Nature-Deficit Disorder* (Chapel Hill, NC: Algonquin Books of Chapel Hill, 2005), 122.

12. Charlotte M. Mason, *Home Education* (London: Kegan Paul, Trench, Trübner, 1920), 61.

13. Michael J. Caduto and Joseph Bruchac, *Keepers of Life: Discovering Plants Through Native American Stories and Earth Activities for Children* (Golden, CO: Fulcrum, 1994), 17.

14. Jamila Norman, interview by Kerry Diamond, *Radio Cherry Bombe*, Newsstand Studios, episode 340, transcript, https://cherrybombe.com /jamila-norman-transcript?rq=jamila%20norman%20transcript.

15. Michael K. Stone and Zenobia Barlow, eds., *Ecological Literacy: Educating Our Children for a Sustainable World* (San Francisco: Sierra Club Books, 2005), 178.

16. Stone and Barlow, *Ecological Literacy*, 179.

17. Stone and Barlow, *Ecological Literacy*, xiii.

18. Stone and Barlow, *Ecological Literacy*, xiv.

19. Stone and Barlow, *Ecological Literacy*, 121.

20. Stone and Barlow, *Ecological Literacy*, 127–29.

21. Robin Wall Kimmerer, *Braiding Sweetgrass for Young Adults: Indigenous Wisdom, Scientific Knowledge, and the Teachings of Plants*, adapted by Monique Gray Smith (Minneapolis: Zest Books, 2022), 10.

Chapter 11: Connection to Others

1. Madeline Levine, *Ready or Not: Preparing Our Kids to Thrive in an Uncertain and Rapidly Changing World* (New York: HarperCollins, 2020), 133.

2. Vito Perrone, *A Letter to Teachers: Reflections on Schooling and the Art of Teaching* (San Francisco: Jossey-Bass, 1991), 4–5.

3. Julie Bogart, *Raising Critical Thinkers: A Parent's Guide to Growing Wise Kids in the Digital Age* (New York: TarcherPerigee, 2022), 90.

4. Bogart, *Raising Critical Thinkers*, 91.

5. Deborah Meier, "The Kindergarten Tradition in the High School," in *Progressive Education for the 1990s: Transforming Practice*, ed. Kathe Jervis and Carol Montag (New York: Teachers College Press, 1991), 147.

6. "New Whiteboard Sessions," Jordan Martino, video, November 21, 2020, https://www.instagram.com/p/CH27Q3xpPBI.

7. Martin Luther King Jr., "The Purpose of Education," in *The Maroon Tiger*, The Martin Luther King, Jr. Research and Education Institute, January 1, 1947, to February 28, 1947, https://kinginstitute.stanford.edu/king-papers /documents/purpose-education.

Index

About the Author

Leslie M. Martino has over twenty years of experience teaching—as an elementary school teacher, a home educator, and an adjunct lecturer for graduate courses focused on the role of the teacher in supporting children's individual work preferences. She homeschools her four children and works as an educational consultant, writing curricula, training teachers, and coaching parents to approach learning in an interest-based and child-directed way. She is a speaker on topics of education and motherhood and is also a contributing writer for the Wild + Free homeschooling community. Leslie enjoys teaching Pilates and collecting nature treasures (though not at the same time). She lives in sunny Florida with her husband and children. You can find her at lesliemartino.com and on Instagram @lesliemmartino.